BALLAD OF DREAMS

Keep Dreaming!

Keep Dreaming!

[signature]

BALLAD OF DREAMS

A NOVEL WITH MUSIC

ALLYSON HERNANDEZ

NEW DEGREE PRESS

BALLAD OF DREAMS
A Novel with Music

ISBN   978-1-63730-642-0 *Paperback*

978-1-63730-725-0 *Kindle Ebook*

978-1-63730-916-2 *Ebook*

*In loving memory of Marie McKenna Bigley
and Laura Kelly Willy.*

*May your stories, resilience, friendship, love of music, theater,
and family live on through the written word and song.*

*"You are never too old, and you are never
too young, to make music."*

CONTENTS

AUDREY

AUTHOR'S NOTE

———

Life is a musical. Life informs music and music informs life. This novel was first born into the world as a musical. You see, I speak fluent musical theater. It's my love language. I studied it in college and followed that dream of Broadway to New York. I spent years pounding the pavement and pursuing my dream, with lots of bumps along the way—success, joy, failure, and frustration. Then I hit a defining moment. I stopped chasing the dream of Broadway and chose a different dream; motherhood.

This book encompasses both of those worlds: theater and motherhood. Much in the way a traditional musical would be structured, there will be dialogue, there will be romance, there will be a heroine chasing after a big dream, and my golly, there will be music! Music? In a book? Yes, well, lyrics. So, imagine you are reading a libretto of a Broadway Musical but with even deeper knowledge into the characters' inner monologues.

So how did this musical/novel get started? Fast forward two decades. My grandmother Marie passed away after ninety-six years of life and two days before my fortieth birthday. Something happens when you turn forty. You start to question everything in your life, such as your values, goals, accomplishments, choices, hopes, and dreams. There was something about turning forty and my grandma passing that lit a huge creative fire in me. Call it a midlife creative crisis.

About two weeks after the funeral, I was on a business trip to Boston for my day job. I had a lot of those questions running through my head, and Grandma was on my mind. I watched Lin-Manuel Miranda's documentary on the plane and listened to him talk about his journey as a writer and how he didn't see himself on Broadway. That was part of his inspiration for writing *In the Heights*. *H*e wanted to create a role only he could fit into.

That's when I had the light bulb moment.

If I were going to write a dream role no one else could play, it would be Grandma. She was a complex, fascinating, and talented woman who lived a big life. And hell, if Lin could do it, why couldn't I? I came home from that Boston trip so inspired and lit up. I wanted to understand what my grandmother wanted in her life. Did she ever want more than motherhood? (She had had thirteen children!) Did she experience the same emotions I did as a forty-year-old wife, mother, and performer? Did she question her life choices when she turned forty?

All of those questions turned into lyrics and melodies that flowed naturally out of me because words and music are imprinted in my brain and my heart. I'd written pop songs before, but never from a character's point of view, and this seemed so much easier. The place, the character, the moment before, all those key components of a musical were starting to take shape.

I worked on the musical for two years and did two readings in New York with some amazingly talented friends. The last reading was at the end of January 2020, a month before the COVID-19 crisis rocked our world and literally shut theater down. Writing became my escape during COVID, and the script took a different direction after three different people in the industry read my script and told me it read like a novel. So, a novel with music was born, flipping the format to meet the times, and breaking all the rules of writing and theater.

Creativity doesn't follow the rules, but even creatives want to put you in a box. They want to define you or your art because that makes it easier for them to understand who you are or what you are. I believe we are not just one thing, and we don't have to fit in a box that someone else defines for us.

Grandma was not *just* a mother. She was not *just* a musician. Neither am I, and neither are you. None of us are just one thing.

As I started the writing process, another character from my childhood came into my mind, my Great Aunt Laura. Aunt Laura lived in NYC in this amazing apartment overlooking Central Park with a pristine baby grand piano in the center of the living room. Her husband Arthur played the piano and was a talent scout. Laura is a big reason I fell in love with New York and theater as she would spoil us growing up by taking us to shows and dinner after.

The idea that I could tell Grandma's story—a Jersey girl with dreams of music, love, motherhood all very similar to my own (okay, I have two children, not thirteen, but still) and of Aunt Laura who never had children and lived in the world of the New York theater scene—really excited me. Two women whose trajectories, choices, sacrifices, and life experiences were so different. Yet here I was, faced with the same life choices and sacrifices as Marie and Laura from the 1940s.

While so much has changed for women since then, so much at the core is still the same.

Both Marie (*renamed Audrey in the book*) and Laura (*renamed Rose*) experienced loss, but loss is not the constant. Their friendship is. They are really the love story here. They both go through a journey of discovering their own identity and independence as women in a time where society and men tried to define that for them.

I've struggled with those definitions myself. I was born a naturally gifted singer, and I've always had a big, powerful voice, even as a little girl. Growing up in church, I was in a children's choir, where I learned how to read music at a young age. I was eight years old when my choir director screamed at me to "blend" because voices are supposed to blend in a choir.

Mine never did.

Over the past year, I discovered the book, *The Genius Habit,* and the author, Laura Garnett, talked about discovering your "core emotional challenge." I realized mine formed all the way back as that little girl in the church choir being told to blend in. I was in the process of writing when I discovered this about myself and turned that into Audrey's character development. That discovery was life changing for me and this story. Her emotional challenge is not to blend in.

I'll be working on not blending in for the rest of my life. It takes guts and courage, but what I've learned in the writing process and through the characters' journeys is this: It's never too late to prioritize yourself, learn who you are, and the many things that make you who you are. We can always choose a new dream or achieve one we thought we never would.

This book is for dream chasers. It's for women, mothers, grandmothers, women in the arts, fathers, grandfathers, brothers, sisters, theater people who love musicals, career-driven performers, musicians, artists, and anyone dealing with their own self-identity, personal discovery, or coping with loss. Out of all the people I just listed, none of them are just one thing. That is exactly why this book is so important. We all need to hear we aren't limited to one path in life.

Ballad of Dreams follows multiple paths, and it demonstrates the shift of how women saw themselves and their identity through different eras of society. It helps readers see how many components can influence and shape our identity while uniquely combining lyrics (music) with novel writing. While inspired by true events and influenced by key moments in history, the story and characters are fictional.

Grandma Marie's Steinway piano is now in my living room in Chatham, New Jersey, and it's a reminder every day she's still here, and she wanted me to write her story, my story, and every woman's story. I've written over twenty songs on Grandma's piano, but there is one closest to my heart: "It's never too late to grab a hold of your dreams. It's never too late to reach for the stars. It's never too late when the sky seems so gray. It's never too late to try."

ACT 1

CHAPTER 1

THANKFUL

AUDREY: JANE'S HOUSE, THANKSGIVING—1992

There are two things I love the most about my family. We are big, and we are loud! To think we take up Jane and Seth's entire Tudor house is astounding to me. With sixty of us, there are tables set in every room of the house just to accommodate us all. Crisp white linens and Rose's antique white china cover the tables. They have an ornate gold border that looks like intricate lace. They were a gift to my daughter Jane from Rose, the day she got married

Jane's house is surprisingly peaceful before the family arrives. The gravy is boiling and gurgling away in the Crock-Pot, familiar scents of chestnut and walnut stuffing fill the air, and the warmth of cinnamon mixed with baked granny smith apples in the oven fills the whole house.

The library, which serves as Seth's office on any day other than Thanksgiving, is to the left of the front door and where the young adults sit—those young adults being my grandchildren. If you are a teenager, college student, or newly married without children, you sit in the library. The formal living room, with its high ceilings of dark mahogany wood, has two round tables set with folding chairs and three long tables in the back of the room for the buffet line. My younger grown children and their spouses—Mary-Catherine and Tony, Ryan and Sunny, Meredith and Danny, Patrick, and Maeve—and all their children typically sit in this room.

Beige and maroon floral couches are in the center of the room, flanked by a long glass and dark wood coffee table. Across from the coffee table is the fireplace that is already crackling, and the smell of smoky wood fills my lungs, emanating warmth throughout the living room. The glass French doors to my left open into a smaller TV room where football will be on later today, and through to the other side of that room, I can see the formal dining room with one long dark wooden table set. That's where I will sit with my boyfriend, Dr. O'Connor, and my oldest children and their spouses. I can already see Dr. O'Connor seated at the table, busily reading a medical journal he picked up from Seth's office.

He happens to look up and catch my gaze, smiles at me, and says, "Audrey, I want to show you something." He motions to me to come over. I grin back quickly but avoid his eyes as I shake my head and point to the door. My children are arriving. I've been avoiding him all day. I can't face him right now. The volume in Jane's house starts to explode with noise as my children and their families start bursting through the front door.

"Hi mom, Happy Thanksgiving!" Helen says as she kisses me on the cheek. "I love that blouse on you. It really brings out your eyes."

"Thank you, dear," I say, kissing and hugging her back.

"Watch out, hot ham and turkey coming through!" Patrick says loudly over the noise, carrying platters of meat through the foyer. "Hi, mom," he says, and air kisses me.

Each one of my children and grandchildren has a little piece of me in them. My daughters all have the same hands as me, and when they stand in a row, their muscular, skinny legs all look identical from behind. My sons have different shades of blue eyes, as do many of their children, and pointy chins, a signature family trait across generations, comes from their grandfather.

Before the meal, we all gather in the foyer wrapped around the dark wooden staircase, and each one of my children says what they are thankful for. Every Thanksgiving, I am reminded of just how incredibly blessed our family is.

"As is tradition, we start with Helen, the oldest," Veronica says, acting as the master of Thanksgiving ceremonies.

"We are so thankful Kendall and Louise are having great semesters at St. E's and Middlebury!" Helen says.

The family claps and cheers. "Keeping the St. Elizabeth's tradition alive," I say. "I'm so proud of both of you."

Robert goes next, "We are thankful Hannah won her soccer tournament this fall and that Matthew's lacrosse team won the state finals. We also welcomed a new furry friend, Elliot, into the family."

"Great name for a dog Robert, and that's wonderful, Hannah and Matthew!" I say, smiling at my grandchildren.

"We're happy to be here this year from Illinois and that the kids got to go to the Macy's Day Parade for the first time this morning. Despite the insane crowds, it was fun," Bernadette says dryly.

"Best parade ever!" some of the grandchildren yell out. The kids continue down the thirteen in birth order, and my cheeks hurt. I'm smiling so wide.

"And last, but certainly not least, our matriarch, mom, would you say grace please?" Veronica says.

"I'm just so thankful to Jane and Seth for graciously hosting us, and I'm so incredibly thankful for all of you. I'm so proud of each of you." I bow my head, "Bless us, O Lord, for these gifts we are about to receive, Amen."

"Amen! Let's eat!" Veronica says, and we all head to our respective tables, grab a plate and eat more than we should.

As I sit down at the table next to Dr. O, he squeezes my hand and says, "I didn't get to say what I was thankful for. I'm thankful for you, Audrey."

"That's very sweet of you, Dr. O. I'm thankful for you too," I say and mean it. I *am* thankful to have another chance at love at this stage in my life. I'm still not ready to give him an answer to the question that could change my life, becoming his wife. I strategically take a big bite of scalloped potatoes and turn to Robert on my left to avoid a longer conversation with Dr. O.

After the buffet dinner, apple and pumpkin pies topped with whipped cream, and my daughter-in-law's adorable turkey-shaped cookies, I take my place at the piano. Music is at the heart of this family. One of my favorite family traditions is to play show tunes and standards, and when the family is tired of singing, I'll play some classical Debussy, Mozart, or Chopin.

Whether it's at my home in Nutley or one of my children's houses, there is usually a piano at the center of the house. If there isn't a piano, then my grandchildren bring a portable keyboard with them to ensure our music traditions carry on regardless of whose house we are at for that holiday. We are spoiled at Jane and Seth's house by a gorgeous black baby grand piano.

As I sit down to play a bit of Debussy, I think about my recent adventures. I've been on a piano treasure hunt around the world, looking for antique and rare pianos. It started with a Wertheim piano in Australia, and then Dr. O and I saw some gorgeous ones in London and Paris. Each one has a story, and I'm fascinated with the history behind them. What kind of house did it live in? Who played it? What type of music did they play on it? Did the piano stay in the family, or was it sold off at auction? Were the keys loved and worn by years of playing music, or have they collected dust sitting untouched and lonely in the corner of a room?

So many unique pianos to find.

Dr. O's silver hair peeks through the glass door to the TV room as he chats with Seth. The two doctors are talking shop, knowing them. He tries to catch my eye as I stare down at the piano keys, still doing all I can to avoid the conversation I know is coming. He's getting impatient, but I'm not ready to give him an answer. I've loved searching for pianos, but I still haven't found *the* piano. The one that will somehow quench my thirst from searching. I'm playing a classic Gershwin, "Someone to Watch Over Me," when I hear my granddaughter, Amelia start singing along as she walks into the living room and sits down next to me on the piano bench.

Amelia is eighteen and has all the fire in her eyes of a dreamer. Her light eyes change shade with what she's wearing, and they are almost turquoise this morning, matching her preppy plaid blazer. She also inherited my gift of music, as did many of my children and grandchildren, but Amelia is pursuing performance just like I did in my youth. I see her drive and talent, and I encourage her as much as I can. With the combination of her long deep brown hair, light eyes, and her gift of music, she reminds me a lot of myself when I was her age. I stop playing to hug her.

"Grandma! Why did you stop? I love this song!" she says. "We were just getting started."

"Is it a crime for wanting to hug my granddaughter when I haven't seen her in months?"

"Of course not," she says with a giggle. "I'm just excited to sing with you today." She takes my hand in hers, gives it a squeeze, and kisses me on the cheek.

"As am I, my dear. And yes, we were just getting started. Let's go back to the bridge where we left off." We finish the song together, and I'm beaming with pride. Amelia's voice is mature, well beyond her eighteen years. It reminds me of the autumn leaves outside, warm, bright, deep, and rich, all at the same time.

"You are so talented, Grandma. I hope I can play the piano as well as you can one day. I wish I never stopped lessons when I was younger. If I only knew how helpful those lessons would be now at Syracuse Drama. Music theory is the hardest. It's all math, and I hate it."

"Oh, don't worry about the math. Theory is all about listening and placement. Listen to what you feel. Where are the notes taking you? Follow the feeling in here." I put my hand on her heart. "You can always get better at the piano. Just keep practicing! You're a girl. You're Irish. You can do anything!"

"I love that! Grandma's spouting girl power. I know I can. It's just this semester..." Amelia looks away, and I can hear the doubt in her voice.

"What is it, dear? What's happening this semester?"

"I tried out for *Carousel* and was psyched to see I got called back for not just one of the leading roles, but for all three."

"That's wonderful! I'm so proud of you!"

"Well, don't be because I didn't get any of them. I'm just in the chorus. "

"You will never *just* be in the chorus to me. What an incredible accomplishment to be considered for all three leading roles! *Carousel* is not an easy show to sing."

"It's not, and I love the music. I think I've played and sang 'What's the Use of Wonderin' to death over the past three months."

"That song never goes out of style," I say.

"Right? I totally agree. The classic musicals from the 1940s fascinate me," Amelia says, her eyes bright with wonder. "Everything seemed so simple then. Girl meets boy, something gets in the way, but they overcome it, and the hero gets what she always wanted, even if she didn't know she wanted it in the first place."

I smile to myself. Life is so much more complicated than the story lines in a musical, but she doesn't know that yet. I nod and listen as the volume in her voice increases with excitement and passion.

"The music, lyrics, and phrasing were simpler too. Maybe it's an old-fashioned way of thinking, but the words of "What's the Use of Wonderin" make so much sense to me," she says as she puts her hand over her heart.

"Music has the power to get right down to the heart of the matter," I say.

"Yes!" Amelia exclaims. "Sometimes, I close my eyes and wish I was living in a 1940s musical. I know it's ridiculous. But you lived it! What was it like, Grandma? What was the theater world really like in the forties?"

"It's natural to romanticize a time period you didn't live through. The ironic thing about history is it does often seem to repeat itself. The forties were a lifetime ago. Do you really want to hear about it?"

"I do. Did you ever audition for shows?"

My memory pulls up the image of rooms filled with women all dressed the same, walking into rooms full of men holding all the power to make our dreams come true.

"I sure did."

"Tell me. Tell me everything." Amelia leans in with eyes wide. I take a deep breath, not knowing exactly where to start except at the beginning, sitting at the piano with my brother Bobby.

CHAPTER 2

WHEN I WAS A GIRL

———

"Being a girl in the 1930s came with certain expectations," I begin. "Expectations I didn't buy into, don't get dirty, don't speak your mind, hide your emotions, and control your temper. Big dreams were only for the boys, so everything was to support the men in your family; cook, clean, wash, iron, repeat."

"Eww, Grandma. I hate all of that!" Amelia exclaims with disgust.

"I did too, but that's what growing up in my childhood home was like back then."

AUDREY'S HOUSE: NUTLEY, NEW JERSEY—1933

It was a tiny house, simple and bare. There was a crucifix hung over the fireplace and a statue of the Virgin Mary on the mantle. In the corner of the living room sat the piano, the only truly fancy piece of furniture we owned and my favorite spot in the house.

Across from the fireplace was dad's powder blue armchair, which was worn and faded. Dad used to sit and smoke in that chair, and the spicy smell of his pipe would often linger in the air long after he'd finished smoking. Right off the living room, connected to the kitchen, was our family dining room.

In the center sat a small dining table that felt too small for the space. A mint green tablecloth covered it. Floral wallpaper hung on the walls, and there was a wooden china cabinet sitting against the far wall with what my mother considered her nicest table settings. The room looked as if the colors used to be bright, but years of living through the Depression had faded them.

For a hardworking, middle-class, Irish Catholic family, I knew we were lucky my dad, Robert, had a job, and for the basic necessities it provided us. As a child, it was easy to forget what my parents handed to me, but the one thing I did not take for granted was the piano. I knew this was a luxury most families would have sold at the peak of the Depression, but luckily, it had been a wedding present to my parents, and something about the pride of that kept them from selling it.

For my parents, our piano wasn't an instrument meant for creating music and bringing joy and life to our house, but more of an extravagant piece of furniture that symbolized our status. My dad wasn't opposed to music though, in fact, we used to huddle by the radio and listen to classical music together often. While he didn't discourage me from playing, he didn't encourage me either.

My mother, Anna, on the other hand, did discourage me. Her only attention toward the piano was when she would make sure it wasn't covered in dust when company came over. I never once saw her try to play it, and my older brother Bobby was so focused on sports he had no interest, so I took my claim of it.

I was about eleven when I started to get the hang of the piano. We couldn't afford music lessons, so I taught myself. One afternoon, I remember practicing my scales diligently, playing and singing: "C, D, E, F, G." As I proudly sang out

"G," a football flew through the air, hitting the piano. You could say I was startled, but Bobby throwing a football in the house was a daily occurrence.

The ever-growing athlete, with smarts as well as talent, was the apple of my parent's eye. His dark, curly brown hair and piercing blue eyes matched mine, and growing up, many people thought we were twins. They weren't entirely wrong. We were Irish twins, born exactly twelve months apart. I worshiped him. His tenacity and athleticism made him a force to be reckoned with, but his thoughtful eyes and charming smile showed his true nature. I didn't just worship him. I wanted to be just like him. Of course, that couldn't happen. He was a son, and I was a daughter.

Bobby sat backward on the piano bench next to me. "Come on, Audrey. Can we play football now? I need someone on my team who can actually catch," he urged.

"And I need someone on my team who can actually listen!" I turned back to the piano and played even louder, hoping my mother would hear me. "C, D, E, F, G, A, B, C!"

"What is all that noise? There are potatoes that need peeling," my mother scolded me from the kitchen.

"She never stops with the potatoes!" I let out an exasperated whine and rolled my eyes at Bobby. He shrugged his shoulders and turned toward the piano.

"Teach me," he said.

I played the scale with my right hand, and he sang out and played with his left hand. Following my example, Bobby sang out, "C, D, E, F, G, A, B, C!" I was surprised by how perfect his pitch was.

My mother walked into the living room and headed toward the piano with a scowl. She was wearing a faded, simple yellow housedress that matched the fabric of the curtains, with a beige cooking apron tied over it. It was her usual domestic uniform, a uniform I did not aspire to be wearing one day.

My mother's frown turned when she heard Bobby singing. "Is there anything you can't do?" she said lovingly, kissing Bobby on the head.

Still vying for her attention and approval, I asked, "Mom, did you hear me?"

"Did you hear me? We have to get dinner ready before your dad gets home from work. The potatoes won't peel themselves."

"I'm sick of peeling potatoes!" I whined. "I want to perform! I'll play the piano and sing at Carnegie Hall in New York City someday!" I declared with all the confidence I had.

"Carnegie Hall? Be sensible, Audrey. You will not waste your time on music." My mother chided. "A woman's place is at home, with her children and caring for her husband." She easily dismissed my dream, replacing it with her current reality as if that was what I wanted for myself. As if she couldn't see anything else for me or my future.

"But mom! I'm not a mother. I'm a kid!" I protested.

"You will be one day, my dear. With that beautiful face and charm, I know you will marry well. Now, learning how to make a delicious pot roast and mashed potatoes is a skill that will serve you well both as a wife and as a mother. Let's go." She grabbed my arm and motioned toward the kitchen, but I squirmed from her grip, refusing to budge from my place at the piano.

She let out an exasperated sigh. "You have five minutes, and then it's time to peel the potatoes," she said as she headed back to the pot roast. I knew my time was short before I'd be made to peel potatoes regardless. Bobby teasingly stuck his tongue out at me, a gesture I returned before turning my attention back to the piano.

"I want to be a mother one day, but I am *not* going to be like her." It was a promise to myself.

With a mischievous twinkle in his eye, Bobby said, "I dare you to carve our initials under the piano."

"Mom would kill us!" I glanced back to the kitchen to see her immersed in her cooking and not paying us any mind. "But it is *our* piano. I bet she won't even notice. Do you have the pocketknife dad gave you?" I asked.

"Sure do," Bobby replied with a wink, taking the knife from his pocket.

"Good." We ducked under the piano together and quietly giggled as Bobby carved his initials first and then handed me the knife to do the same.

"There! A. M. and R. M.," Bobby whispered proudly.

"It's perfect." I admired our handy work, fingers tracing the carved letters on the wood. "One day, Bobby, people will know us, and it won't be for peeling potatoes!" I said, thinking I could just will it into truth. I climbed out from under the piano, daydreaming of my future as I started to sing to Bobby, using the living room as my stage.

I Want More

AUDREY
I'll be the perfect essence of charm and grace
An Irish girl with champagne taste
I'll be All-Day Rich and Rosy
and everyone will know me
But I'll want more

More than I can ever wish for
More than what the future has in store
I want more
I want more
I want more

I'll be applauded by
adoring fans as they pass by
and there's no reason why
I can't touch the sky

I'll be the perfect essence of charm and grace
an Irish girl with champagne taste
I'll be All-Day Rich and Rosy
and everyone will love me
but I'll want more

I belted out the end of the song, standing on top of the piano bench and arms straight up in a big jazz-hands finish. With my arms still in the air, Bobby threw the football at me, and I caught it easily.

"You know Audrey, if you stop searching for more, you might find you already have all you need," said Bobby, with that older brother, 'know it all' logic.

"Bobby, you will *never* understand what it's like to be a girl."

"Nor would I want to! Besides, you're not a *girl*. You're my *sister*."

"Ha! Well, right now, this *sister* is gonna beat you at this game! I'm a girl, I'm Irish, I can do anything!" I replied, gazing down on him from my perch and feeling taller and more important for once.

We were halfway to the front door, football in hand, and thinking I would be able to escape potato peeling when my mom stopped me dead in my tracks. "Audrey, where do you think you're going?" My mother asked.

"Bobby and I are going to …"

"No, *Bobby* can go play outside. You have potatoes to peel."

Free as a bird, Bobby flew out the door while I was trapped in a cage, wishing we could trade places.

CHAPTER 3

NEVER BE PERFECT

———

I'm not sure who put more pressure on Bobby and me, our parents or ourselves?

I had fought against the grain my whole childhood, wanting to catch up with the boys, wanting to make my parents proud, and wrestling with not blending in. We come from an Irish family that values hard work and winning. Failing is not really in our genetic makeup.

But I remember a big failure for myself during my college years while singing with my college choir at St. Elizabeth's. My choir director, Sister Pious, and I, well, let's just say we had words. We disagreed about the difference between having a powerful voice and needing to conform to her musical standards. She was a purist when it came to classical music and always praised the sopranos with their perfect pitch and airy high notes.

She never liked me. I didn't blend, *and* I didn't keep my opinions to myself. But I loved to sing, and harmonies just came naturally to me.

SETON HALL UNIVERSITY, SPRING—1941

I was meeting Bobby at Faegan's, a local college bar on campus. The crowded bar smelled of sweat, was filled with a haze of smoke, and my heels stuck to the floor from a layer of spilled beers. I hated this bar, but it was Bobby's stomping ground. I missed my brother and needed to talk to him about what had happened at my college, so there I was.

That evening, the bar was divided into two very distinct groups, much like the world we were living in. The football players and other jocks were on one side of the bar, huddled around a radio listening to a local game and glued to the play-by-play of the announcers. On the other side of the bar were the intellectuals and political like-minded, listening to the news and debating the biased coverage. Between them sat Bobby, acting as a bridge to both worlds.

While many of his teammates were flirting with a crowd of adoring young fans, Bobby was in his own little world, oblivious to the beautiful young women desperately trying to get his attention. The cheerful blue and white Seton Hall University Football jerseys and the youthful energy of the crowd was a stark contrast to Bobby, who was sitting by the bar alone, listening intently to the radio. Charles Lindbergh, a political activist of The America First Committee, was giving a speech.

"No person of honesty and vision can look on their pro-war policy here today without seeing the dangers involved in such a policy, both for them and for us. Instead of agitating for war, the Jewish groups in this country should be opposing it in every possible way, for they will be among the first to feel its consequences. A few farsighted Jewish people realize this and stand opposed to intervention. But the majority still do not"

(CHARLESLINDBERGH.COM, AMERICA FIRST)

Bobby leaned in and debated to both the radio and the mix of athletes, fans, and intellectuals sitting at the bar. "So Americans and Jewish Americans should ignore the atrocities being done to the Jewish people in Europe while our country has the means to intervene?"

I took note of the young women with admiration and stars in their eyes, the teammates who couldn't care less but still listened to him as the team captain, and the intellectuals who nodded along in agreement. He had many of them in the palm of his hand, showing how he was truly a natural leader. He always had been.

"Talking to the radio again, Bobby?" I said with a smile.

"Audrey, you made it. Sorry, you know how Lindbergh gets my blood boiling." His intensity softened when he saw me and leaned in to give me a hug.

"Nothing to apologize for. I admire your passion," I said with an immense amount of pride, and he gave me a huge smile.

"Thanks, Audrey."

"I said I admire your passion. I didn't say I agree with you."

"You have got to be kidding me. Do you know what's going on in the world? How can you agree with Lindbergh?"

"I know how you feel, Bobby, but I just don't see why the US needs to get involved. It's not our fight."

"You are so wrong, Audrey. We are a country that stands for liberty, freedom, and that all men are created equal. How can a country built on those beliefs ignore the evilest attempt in the world to eradicate a group of people simply based on their ethnic and religious background?"

"I see your point, but honestly, Bobby, I'm sick of all this war talk. I want to hear music and comedy on the radio. Let the world powers work it out *off* the air. How am I supposed to know my competition if I can't listen to the latest talent?"

"It's ridiculous if you think wars are just 'worked out,' Audrey. The radio is not just for music, and the news is important," he sighed. "I need another drink." He ordered two beers from the bartender, took a big gulp from one, and handed me the other.

I looked at it with judgment in my eyes and motioned to the bartender. "Do you happen to have champagne?"

The bartender rolled his eyes at me. "This is not that kinda bar doll." I shrugged my shoulders, looked at the beer, and thought, *why not,* and took a big gulp of the beer.

Bobby's eyes widen. "Oh boy, what happened?"

"Sister Pious happened. In the middle of choir practice, she turned and yelled at me, *"Audrey! Blend!"*

"Don't let her get under your skin," he replied. I shook my head because it was easier said than done.

"I can't help it. I'm loud. I don't blend," I said. I was never able to blend in most aspects. I didn't blend into crowds, I stuck out among other girls, and I certainly didn't sound like the other girls in the choir. My voice was more powerful by a long shot, and it was hard to control the volume because that's just how my voice was.

"No, you don't. So why do you care?" Bobby confirmed what I was thinking, but I did care. I still wanted to be liked, accepted, and my talent validated, just like everyone else.

"Well, I said to her, 'I don't blend!' She proceeded to tell me to stop dreaming of the stage because I was never gonna make it anyway, and then kicked me out of the choir!" I exclaimed, getting angrier and angrier as I relived the moment.

"I'm so sorry. One day you'll look back on this and laugh. Besides, there are more important things going on in the world." Bobby consoled me, trying to lighten the mood, but my mind was still very much on the present and not on the future.

"But maybe she's right. Who do I think I am anyway? I'm no star Bobby, I'm just an Irish girl from Jersey," I replied sadly. Bobby grabbed both of my shoulders, bracing me for one of his pep talks.

"You're much more than that, Audrey. You're a McKenna. You're not supposed to blend in! How many times did you practice Fur Elise growing up until it was perfect without ever taking a lesson? Or when you beat Nancy Crowley for Student Council President, who was a shoo-in to win? Or when you broke your arm on stage and insisted on singing through the pain before going to the hospital?"

"I guess I forgot," I mumbled, staring at him intently. "You're always so confident. Do you ever feel like no matter how hard you try, you'll never live up to what other people want you to be?" I questioned, thinking there was no way Bobby ever felt so self-conscious.

Bobby surprised me when he smiled and replied, "Every day."

Never Be Perfect

BOBBY
I can hear dad's voice in my head
When I'm out on the field
Win at all costs
only losers will yield
So I train harder, I run faster
I feel the win on my heels
and when I win
I see you in the stands
Mom proudly clapping her hands,
You are our golden boy

Handsome, smart and strong
Your future will be our greatest joy

But what if I lose?
What if I'm not fast enough?
What if I'm not smart enough?
What if I lose?
Who's the golden boy then?

I'll never be perfect
I'll never be who you want me to be
I'll never be perfect
The pressure is there, and it's all I can see
I'll never be perfect

AUDREY
I can hear mom's voice in my head,
getting ready for the dance
Keep your waist small
pretty girls find romance
So I primp longer, I smile wider
I put on my lipstick and heels
and when I'm done
and walk down the stairs
Mom proudly fixes my hair,
You are our golden girl
Beauty, brains and charm
Your future will be our greatest joy

AUDREY/BOBBY
But what if we lose?
What if we're not fast enough?

What if we're not smart enough?
What if we lose?

BOBBY
Who's the golden boy?

AUDREY
Who's the golden girl then?

AUDREY/BOBBY
We'll never be perfect
We'll never be who they want us to be
We'll never be perfect
The pressure is there, and it's all we can see
We'll never be perfect

AUDREY/BOBBY
Together, imperfect we will be

"We might not be perfect, Audrey, but if there is one thing I know, it's that nothing can stop us." Bobby took my chin in his hand and lifted it up. Our tender moment turned into a rallying cry and one we reminded each other of often into the future.

"Nothing can stop the McKenna's. We make a goal and get out of our way." I smiled, knowing just how lucky I was to have the best big brother.

Nothing could stop us when we had each other, and we all felt unstoppable that summer at the beach. We had no idea what was coming.

CHAPTER 4

THE SUMMER OF 1941

AUDREY: LONG BRANCH BEACH, NEW JERSEY—1941, PART ONE

My guy friends didn't apologize for who they were or what they wanted, and I loved that about them. They aggressively competed in sports, in smarts, and in life. Growing up with Bobby, everything was a competition, and being with our crew of friends, Ted and Vic, I guess you could say they brought out the fire in me. My cousin Rose was the one friend who balanced me out and brought me back down to earth, reminding me of my more feminine side, but sometimes I didn't want to be diplomatic and feminine. I just wanted to be one of the guys and say and do whatever I wanted without consequences or judgment of being too brash or bold.

Bobby and I often spent our summers in Rumson, New Jersey, as my uncle Joseph had a house there he generously let us visit every summer, and that summer was no different. I was a bright and shiny young woman of twenty-one, and Bobby a year older. Dad had to work and wouldn't be down until the weekend, and my mom had let us go down on our own ahead of them, with the strict instructions that, "Your brother Bobby is in charge." As much as I wanted to complain about it, I didn't. I knew we were lucky to get out of Nutley and go to the beach.

My uncle Joseph was waiting for us when we arrived. He was always kind to Bobby and me and treated us like we were his own. As the young adults we were that summer, Uncle Joseph gave us the freedom to make ourselves at home and come and go as we pleased. He had even handed Bobby a beer when we got there to toast the new summer season.

As soon as Bobby and I unloaded our stuff, I changed into a red summer dress, and we headed to the beach in the late afternoon. I loved the time of day when the sun was just starting to set, and families had already gone home for dinner. But despite the lack of families, the Long Branch Boardwalk was still bustling with food vendors and games, young men walking hand-in-hand with their sweethearts, and children begging their moms for a balloon or an ice cream on their way home.

Down on the sand was where young couples snuggled up on blankets while groups of friends drank beer and played football. That's what I wanted to do with my friends, and it seemed like everyone I knew was there. Bobby, Ted, and Vic were thick as thieves and had been close friends since childhood. Ted had a stocky, athletic build from years of playing football with Bobby and sandy blond hair that often flopped in front of his glasses. He had the awkward charm of a young Clark Kent. Bobby and Ted were talking down by the water while we all waited for Vic.

I was anxious for Vic to arrive as we had just started dating a few months prior, and it always felt like I was floating on air whenever he was near. I was doing some stretches and getting ready to play football with the boys when Ted said, "You're wearing a dress."

"So!" I said with exasperation.

"It's football Audrey, not one of your concerts with your boyfriend, Vic." His voice dripped with sarcasm.

"I can play football and sing with Vic. It's called being well-rounded." Ted was always making jokes, and they were usually funny, but I wasn't laughing this time. I had no patience for traditional thinking of what I could or could not do as a woman.

"I was joking."

"I wasn't."

"Clearly. Bobby will not be happy if I let something happen to his kid sister." Ted paused and asked sincerely, "What if you get hurt?"

"What if *you* get hurt?" I teasingly made a fist and got closer to Ted's face like I was about to punch him. Ted pulled my hand down, brought his face close to mine, and there was a brief moment of tension. I couldn't put my finger on Ted's expression, but I knew it made my stomach flip. I could never quite pinpoint what laid behind those eyes.

"Hey! Are we gonna play some football or what?" Vic yelled from across the beach, breaking the tension.

I quickly pulled away from Ted and ran to Vic. His olive complexion and thick jet-black hair looked even darker against his white T-shirt, a drastic contrast to my own pale and freckled skin. His parents had both been born in Sicily before immigrating to the US. Not only was he first generation, but he was also the first in their family to finish high school and go to college, two facts they were very proud of.

The combination of his amber-brown eyes, long eyelashes, and matching dimples that appeared in each cheek when he smiled made me swoon. I jumped into his arms and kissed him like no one else was watching. His strong arms enveloped me, and I was completely lost in the moment until I heard the snickers from Ted and Bobby.

"Ted's afraid I'll get hurt playing football." I was annoyed but also fully aware I was playing the damsel in distress.

Vic raised his eyebrows and said, "You might." He picked me up and swung me around in the air. My red and white dress twirled, and I felt as light as a feather. "Then I'd have to carry you home." As he lowered me down to the ground, he teased, "You better not play."

"You boys don't want me to play because you don't want to lose." Vic and Ted both looked at each other and shook their heads.

A football flew through the air as I heard Bobby yell, "Audrey, think fast!" I caught it, gave Ted and Vic a 'told you so' look, and then threw the football back to Bobby. Bobby smiled, his face covered in little brown freckles from a summer in the sun.

I started running, turned my head, and yelled back to the boys, "Race you to the pier!"

"Race or chase?" Vic flirted back at me with a knowing glance. I sprinted as fast as I could in the sand and quickly looked back to see Ted, Vic, and Bobby running behind me. Just when I was ready to beat them all, Bobby caught up quickly and won. I came in second while Vic and Ted tied for last place. We were all out of breath, except for Bobby, who didn't even seem winded.

"We just got beat by a girl!" Vic whined.

"McKenna's are fast," Bobby replied.

"And we hate to lose!" I added.

Ted and Vic were now both rolling their eyes at Bobby and me. Then Vic said with his best radio advertisement voice, "The world's greatest family—where girls play football and boys become presidents." Ted and Vic laughed. Bobby winked at me, and at that moment, we were those little kids under the piano again dreaming of more.

"Bobby will be the next FDR," Ted said with conviction.

"Maybe I'll be the next FDR. Who says a woman can't run for president?" The boy's laughter answered the question. I knew they'd laugh, but I couldn't understand why it was ridiculous to assume women could do the same important things men could. "Hey! It could happen one day! Jeannette Rankin in Montana, she's in Congress!"

"All right, enough, Audrey. Leave the politics to me, please." Bobby shut me down, reminding me yet again he was the older, 'wiser' brother.

Vic grabbed my hand and squeezed it, whispering in my ear, "If anyone can do it, it's you, Audrey. Determination looks good on you." He kissed me on the cheek, and I knew I was blushing.

"I'm starving! Let's go grab a hot dog," Bobby announced, interrupting the moment between Vic and me.

I didn't think Bobby necessarily disapproved of Vic and me—Vic was one of his best friends—but I was pretty sure he didn't like it or me having a boyfriend at all. The first time Vic took me out for a milkshake, Bobby had gone to the same diner. He sat in a booth a few rows down with Ted and a few other friends from college and had managed to be sitting on our front porch at the exact moment Vic dropped me off. Coincidence or an overprotective brother?

"You buying, Mr. President?" Ted asked.

"Sure. Gambled your last buck away again, Ted?" joked Bobby.

"I was robbed!" exclaimed Ted.

"And in walks Bobby, saving the day again," Vic said.

Bobby and Ted started walking toward the boardwalk. Bobby, highly aware Vic and I would be alone together on the beach, asked a question that sounded more like a statement, "Audrey, you coming?"

"Let me just grab my sweater. I left it back there," I replied. As I saw Bobby's disapproving eyes, I quickly ran back to grab my sweater. I looked back at the others, who were both my close friends *and* my family, and could see how carefree their lives seemed. No one gave it a second thought what they were wearing if they were alone on the beach with a girl or what time they arrived home.

I was suddenly very aware I was the only woman with a group of three guys. I didn't like the stares of the other women on the beach making assumptions about me and sighed, wishing Rose was there to share in my woes. She would understand how I felt. Before I could wallow in my self-pity for too long, Vic walked up to me, having ditched Bobby and Ted to come to keep me company. I smiled at him, choosing instead to enjoy my time with him than lament about being a woman.

Bobby and Ted had gone far ahead of us, so Vic and I finally had a moment alone. We walked hand-in-hand on the beach without a care in the world. A white seashell caught my eye, and I crouched down in the sand to pick it up. To my surprise, it was the most perfect starfish. I held it in the palm of my hand, when Vic leaned in and kissed me with confidence as smooth and delicious as chocolate ice cream on a hot summer day. As I held the starfish, I felt like I was see-ing stars in my eye*s and* in the sand. I lingered a second too long and then pulled away to compose myself. I turned my head away from his eyes and looked down at the sand, trying to hide everything I was feeling, but I couldn't stop smiling.

"Tell me you love me," he whispered against my ear.

"You know I do."

"And I'm the lucky fella who gets to love you." Vic grinned wide, his usual devilish look gleaming in his eyes. It was a look I couldn't resist. I found his cockiness to be rather charming, and if he could be bold, then so could I.

I took a deep breath and blurted out, "I don't think I've ever wanted someone as much as I want you."

"Yeah?" He winked at me and then ran his fingers through my hair. "What else do you want?"

"I want music, I want love, and I want children! I want it all!"

I Want More

AUDREY

I'll be the perfect essence of charm and grace
An Irish girl with Champagne taste
I'll be All-Day Rich and Rosy
And everyone will know me

"Everyone will know you, Audrey! They will know us! We will be quite the musical duo, what with your voice and talent at the piano and my musical prowess and charming, good looks? We'll be unstoppable!" I shook my head, laughing at how sure of himself he was. If there was one thing Vic did not lack, it was confidence.

"Humility is one of your best qualities," I joked.

"Who needs humility when you have talent like ours? I see concerts and shows with people lined up around the block to buy tickets."

"Oh Vic, can you imagine? Carnegie Hall, with you in a tux and me in a gorgeous gown?"

"A blue gown. You should always wear blue. It makes your eyes sparkle." He knew just what to say. He stole another kiss so fast I wasn't expecting it, but then it was slow and smooth, and I was melting again.

"The whole world is ahead of us, waiting for us," he said as he picked me up and spun me around.

"Like one big song to be sung." He was quiet for a minute, and I could see the wheels turning in his head.

"Why do you love music so much?" he asked.

"It makes me feel alive like it's what I was born to do."

"Me too. Music is in my blood."

"That's why you understand me. You get that life without music is simply—"

"Gray," he finished my thought.

"Yes! It's music that brings out all the colors of the rainbow."

"I wonder if music were a color, what color would it be?"

The Color is You

VIC
Shades of blue
Hues of violet
Flashes of green
Whispers of yellow

AUDREY
Don't forget red
Oh, you go to my head
Strawberry, Cherry, Crimson
There's a shade for every season

VIC

And a sound for every reason
Why I love you...
I love you

AUDREY

like a Chopin concerto
like a Porter up-tempo
like a Gershwin glissando
like a Mozart allegro

VIC

Like a resting fermata
A mighty orchestra
a somber rallentando
Like a booming fortissimo

VIC & AUDREY

And if music was a color
The color is you
You give the music so much color
There's only music with you

AUDREY

I love you
Like a Vibrant vibrato
Like a Shining soprano

VIC

Like a Fiery falsetto
Like a Classy Cool contralto

AUDREY

A classy contralto!

VIC

Relax, you know I'm a mezzo kinda guy.

AUDREY

Like the pink of a peony
The timbre of a symphony

VIC

The orange of a sunset
The rhythm of a trip-el-let

VIC & AUDREY

And if music was a color
The color is you
Without you, there is no color
There's only music with you
And if music was a color

VIC

The color is blue

AUDREY

No—the color is RED

VIC

Isn't that what I said?

AUDREY

You said the color is blue

VIC
No, the color is you

AUDREY & VIC
The Color is You

"Do you really think we can make it as a duo act?" I questioned honestly.

"We've got chemistry. Any producer would be a fool not to see that! We should go to the next audition Carnegie has for new acts."

"I don't know if I'm ready for that Vic, I just got kicked out of the choir." Sister Pious had been pretty clear I didn't blend in. If I couldn't make it in a college choir, how on earth would I be able to make it at Carnegie? Maybe with Vic as my partner, it would be different? Our voices did blend beautifully together. We both had powerful voices, but together they wove in and out intricately, balancing each other and maximizing our power and sound.

"You can do this, Audrey. We can do this." Vic believed in me, and that was all that mattered. I was scared, but I knew I wouldn't be doing it alone.

"I'll practice till my fingers bleed if that's what it takes!"

He took my hands in his and kissed my fingers like they were a bouquet of tulips. "That's my girl!" I jumped into his arms and screamed with excitement.

This was really happening!

CHAPTER 5

THE GOOD OLD DAYS

AUDREY: LONG BRANCH BOARDWALK, NEW JERSEY—1941, PART TWO

It had gotten dark, around ten o'clock at night. Vic and I had just left the beach and were on our way to find the rest of the gang because I knew Bobby would be wondering what took us so long. As we strolled down the boardwalk holding hands, we saw other young couples in love soaking in the last moments of summer, and I understood how they felt. You just didn't want summer to end. Freeze time, freeze the warm summer nights walking hand in hand, where nothing else mattered except how that person looked at you.

Bobby was waiting for us outside the Irish pub, but before he could even ask where we had been, we saw Ted holding a huge, light brown Teddy bear dressed in a pink dress with a white bow around its neck.

"Winning big over at the ring toss, I see," I said to Ted.

"You didn't have any better prize options, huh?" Vic asked.

"I kinda lost a bet," Ted said, looking down at his feet.

"Never make a bet with a McKenna," I teasingly whispered to Ted. He knew better than to make a bet with

Bobby because Bobby always won. Ted clearly didn't appreciate me pointing that out to him, though, and rolled his eyes.

Bobby held up the bear as if it was a real woman and said, "I'd like to introduce you all to Ted's date for the night, Miss Ted E. Bear!"

"Nice to meet you, Ma'am," Vic said and shook the bear's hand.

"So glad you could join us," I said as if welcoming the bear into our group of friends for the night.

"Ted, what do you think? You think the pub will let you in with a bear on your arm?" Bobby asked jokingly.

Ted started to lighten up and addressed the bear like she was his date for the night. "What do you think, doll? Care for a drink?"

"The bear is better looking than your last girlfriend, Ted!" Vic pointed out with a hearty laugh, and then Bobby laughed along with him. I didn't laugh along.

I remembered Ted's last girlfriend, Millie. She was a sweetheart, and Ted really seemed to like her until the guys gave him a hard time about her plain looks. While usually a good guy with a good sense of humor about things, Ted had let them get under his skin more than he should have and ended up dumping the poor girl.

Ted cringed and said, "Laugh all you want. I have to hold the bear, but the first round's on Bobby."

"Sounds good to me," Vic said approvingly.

"Bobby, I forgot to tell you something," I said, changing the subject. "We have some exciting news to share. Vic and I are going to audition to be a duo act at Carnegie Hall!"

Bobby seemed suddenly relieved at the news as if he'd been expecting something else, and I wondered what he thought I was going to say. I didn't dwell on the thought long as he smiled warmly at me.

"That's great! We'll be in the front row cheering you on, won't we, Ted?" he said.

"Sure. I love listening to Audrey sing," Ted answered shyly, looking at his feet again and then up at me quickly. I was so focused on the goal in front of me I didn't even say thank you.

"I'm going to start practicing for our audition early tomorrow. Vic, you should stop by the house tomorrow at noon, and we'll rehearse. You boys have fun tonight! Don't get into too much trouble!" I kissed Vic on the cheek and started to leave.

I heard Ted cheer out a devious, "Trouble here we come!" and turned to watch the three of them walk into the pub.

I'd be lying if I said I didn't want to stay myself. Why couldn't I stay out late and cause some trouble? Why did Vic get to stay and drink with his friends while I needed to go home, sleep, and practice even more than he did? So, instead of going home, I turned on my heel and followed the boys into the pub.

The Irish pub had a long, dark cherry wood bar with wooden bar stools, a pool table in the corner, and a game of darts hanging on the wall. I spotted the boys at the bar, and before they could spot me, I headed toward the ladies' room in the back of the pub and positioned myself behind a big potted plant outside the door. I needed to know what they were up to.

Ted put the bear in a chair next to him as Bobby leaned over the bar to talk to the bartender. "Three pints, please. Oh, and an extra one for the doll," Bobby said, motioning to the bear. The boys all laughed, and once they got their beers, they chugged them down. That round was followed by another and then another.

By their fourth round, they started playing darts, and the three of them started singing like a bunch of drunken fools. If I had ever drunk that much, I would have never heard the end of it from Bobby. But the three of them were like brothers, and they had their own rules. I couldn't even imagine the trouble they had gotten into when I wasn't around.

The Good Old Days

BOBBY
It was the summer at camp Columbus
without a care in the world
best friends as camp counselors
we spent every day outdoors

TED
The air was fresh and crisp

VIC
The lake was cool and clean

BOBBY
We swam until our legs ached

BOBBY, TED, VIC
Drank cold beer in the canteen

The three of them chugged their beers with such gusto. I was almost impressed. Vic had a little foam mustache forming above his upper lip, and I had to stop myself from giggling. He looked so cute. Then Bobby, Ted, and Vic let out a synchronized burp, laughed, and slapped each other on the back with pride. I didn't understand boys, but they were clearly having a great time and were so unencumbered.

They didn't seem to be worrying at all about what the people around them thought. How refreshing.

Rose and I could never behave like that in public, though the image of Rose and I burping in public had me giggling again. I didn't think Rose was even capable of something so inelegant. The boys had linked their arms around each other and were swaying back and forth, jostling their beers and spilling some on the already sticky floor.

BOBBY, TED, VIC
Oh, I remember it well
So many stories to tell
of the good old days
the good old days

VIC
We woke up by the morning sun
Threw on our shoes, went for a run

BOBBY
Played a game of football
made bonfires at nightfall

TED
Vic would sing us songs
And we'd all sing along

VIC
Ted playing darts and placing bets

TED
Bobby playing hard to get

TED, BOBBY, VIC
The pranks we used to play
seemed to get funnier every day
we were like brother's people would say
if we could only go back and stay
We'd flirt with all the girls
The blond one with the curls
The redhead with the green eyes
The brunette with the killer thighs

TED, BOBBY, VIC
Oh, we'll remember this well
So many stories to tell
Of these good, these good old days
These are the good
Cheers to these good
These good old days!

Of course, there were other girls that previous summer. Those were the good old days for them. I was working my tail off at a girls' camp, where we had a curfew every night. I got stuck on kitchen duty while they had been living it up at the boys' camp. But as much as I wanted to be angry with them, I couldn't help but see them all for who they were; carefree best friends whom I loved.

As I snuck my way out of the bar, careful not to be seen, I looked back to see the three of them still arm in arm, each with their steins of beer in hand, smiling from ear to ear and framed like a perfect photograph.

AUDREY'S HOUSE: FALL—1941

As summer came to a close, all I did was practice, practice, and then practice again. I was trying to get ready for the big audition and my cousin Rose was there helping me prepare. Her delicate frame and long fingers had served her well the years she sewed costumes with her mother Sadie at a Broadway Theater before she had married her husband, Oscar.

Oscar was a talent scout, and the two of them met at the theater. She'd been a young woman of twenty at the time, and Oscar being five years her senior, had charmed her right off her feet. Not that I could fault her for being so easily charmed. Oscar was tall with an elegant air about him in how he stood, walked, and even spoke. His voice could command a stage with little issue, and he was a very warm and generous sort of person. He adored Rose, and Rose adored him. They made for a classy New York couple.

Rose was a vision of class in her blush pink dress, tailored to perfection, which accentuated how lean she was in comparison to my curves. Her caramel brown hair, almost a strawberry blond depending on the light, perfectly accented her pale blue eyes. Everything about Rose, in both demeanor and appearance, was softer and lighter than me.

I had been trying to practice, but I kept getting distracted by my daydreams of Vic. My fingers were just tripping over themselves because my mind was on his hands, lips, mouth, and voice… shoot! There I'd gone again, messing up the notes and stopping mid-song.

"Ugh! I can't seem to get that one part right. Let me try it again," I complained to Rose.

"I thought it sounded wonderful!" Rose replied.

"Oh, you're just saying that."

"I wouldn't say it if I didn't mean it."

"Okay, well, thank you. I just need to keep practicing that one section, I suppose."

"Why don't you take a break and tell me all about this new beau of yours. Are you in love with him?"

Leave it to Rose to get right to the heart of the matter and ask me the hard questions. She had always been my voice of reason and the friend that knew what I was thinking before I said it.

I had thought I could keep my thoughts to myself, but I guess I hadn't hidden them as well as I thought I had. "Is it that obvious?"

"Well, yes, but it's a beautiful thing to be young and in love! I remember when Oscar and I were courting. Kissing became our new sport! We couldn't keep our hands off of each other!"

"Rose!" I said, surprised, blushing. It wasn't like her to talk about such things with me, intimate things, I mean. She was five years older than me, and I honestly didn't remember when she and Oscar had courted. They'd never been very affectionate in public, though I had known they loved each other just from their energy when they were together.

Oscar had a deep respect for Rose and listened to her opinions like she wasn't just his wife but his partner. He lavished her with everything from jewelry to fur gowns, fancy dinners, and show tickets. There had been a lot of love between them, but passion? I wouldn't have said passion.

Now Vic and I, on the other hand, it had been like a powerful force pulling us together, both physically and emotionally. Being around Vic was like getting so close to a fire you could get burned if you got any closer.

Rose and Oscar were also older than us and had been married for several years, so there was a maturity and wisdom they exuded. I wondered what they had been like when they first started dating. Did the passion fade the longer they were married? It was really none of my business what went on behind closed doors, but as an unmarried woman, I was curious. What would marriage be like for me?

"What?" She gave me a cheeky smile. "Well?" She was determined to get it out of me.

Mr. Butter

AUDREY
All he has to do is look at me
Those dark steamy eyes
and that voice
It's like butter-melting
and I'm-toast.

Mr. Butter melted my…
Ooh, Mr. Butter
Oooh Oohh Ooh Mr. Butter
Please won't you melt my…

"Do you think he will propose?" Rose asked with wide eyes, hanging on my every word. She leaned in and took my hands in hers, living vicariously through my romantic description.

"I hope he will. We'll make music together, and when we're tired of show biz, we'll settle down and have a bunch of kids. I'll have a life full of love and music."

That was the dream right there. Music, love, *and* a family. I pictured each of our children being more musical than the last, with dark hair and blue eyes. They would be the most gorgeous combination of both of us, and at night, we'd all sit by the fire and sing to each other.

AUDREY
All he has to do is wink at me
That dark flowing hair
And those lips
They're like butter melting
And I'm toast.

AUDREY
Mr. Butter melted my...

AUDREY & ROSE
Ooh, Mr. Butter
Oooh Oohh Ooh Mr. Butter
Please won't you melt my...

AUDREY
I'm Toast.

We exploded into giggles and could not stop laughing, like two little school girls talking about their first crushes. I could feel my face was all flushed from just thinking about him, and my heart was pounding out of my chest. That was what he did to me! I was putty in his hands, and he wasn't even there.

I desired him. That's what that was, right? Pure and utter desire? Or was that what love did to you? I was a good

Catholic girl, and I knew lust was wrong but was it lust if you loved each other? It was a good thing Rose couldn't read my thoughts, though I wondered if she could see them on my face. How embarrassing.

"I can picture us all out on the town, two classy and talented couples. We'll be the envy of the New York theater scene. I think dress shopping is in order!" Rose painted a glamorous picture. In it, I was floating through the streets of New York, and everyone was looking and pointing at us. How could they not? We'd be dressed to the nines and looking like royalty. He'd treat me like a queen, and I would be his equal both onstage and off.

"Audition dress shopping, yes," I corrected her.

"You *must* wear red. We'll make you look as fashionable as the stars in "Lady in the Dark!" Rose gushed. I did love red, but I knew Vic loved me in blue. Though I was sure, he'd love me in red just the same, whatever made me happy, right?

"I haven't seen that show yet!"

"I'll tell Oscar to get tickets for the four of us. It'll be an early engagement present."

"Mr. Butter hasn't proposed yet."

"Oh, but he will!" Rose trilled, grabbing me in a huge hug and jumping up and down. She seemed so sure, and I could only hope she was right.

Why wouldn't he propose? He would be a fool not to ask me! If only women could have done the asking then, I would have had it locked up weeks prior, and I would have been planning a wedding instead of dreaming of one. I wondered if he'd sing to me on our wedding day. Oh, that would be so romantic. If I closed my eyes, I could just hear the beautiful music we'd make together.

CHAPTER 6

NIGHTS AT THE THEATER WITH OSCAR

———

ROSE: THANKSGIVING, JANE'S HOUSE—1992

My fingers gently dust the intricate gold rim of my china that Jane has set on the tables. I think of Oscar fondly, and the nights we ate our usual dinner on these plates, and I can still taste the peaches and rye bread like it was yesterday. I haven't thought about that in years, but seeing Amelia so taken with her grandmother's story not only touches my heart but has made me want to tell her mine too.

I wander over to Audrey and Amelia as Audrey comes to a pause in sharing her memories, and I can't help reminiscing with her. "The men held all the power while we had to just wait for them to make decisions. It was a different reality for women when we were young. You can't even fathom Amelia," I say, picking up where Audrey left off.

"Like what?" Amelia asks.

"Well, for one, I couldn't even open my own bank account without a man in 1941," Audrey says.

"That's crazy! What were you supposed to do?" Amelia asks.

"Depend on our husband," I reply. "Uncle Oscar always took care of the money, and me, for a long time."

"I remember having this same conversation before. If memory serves correctly, I reminded you not to take him for granted," Audrey says.

"We would joke with each other, 'You're a girl, you're Irish,'" I say.

"You can do anything!' Except open a bank account!" Audrey and I say together, laughing.

It really wasn't funny, though. We didn't have a lot of choices back then, and the choices we did make would change the course of our lives.

I know mine did.

ROSE AND OSCAR'S APARTMENT, NEW YORK—1942

It was a Friday night. The night Oscar and I would go to the theater to see a new show. It was always my favorite night of the week because it felt like going home. I practically grew up backstage and always loved the costumes. I admired the craftsmanship that went into them and learned from my seamstress mother, helping her just to make ends meet.

I used to love running my fingers through the new fabrics when we built costumes from scratch. A piece of green silk could magically transform into a gorgeous dress fit for a queen, a pile of silver sequins could elevate the drabbest old dress into a sparkly showstopper, and royal blue wool could become a form-fitting suit for a leading man. It was always so satisfying to see the final product after days of sewing.

Working in the theater world was a big part of my family's life. While my mom and I worked behind the scenes, my sister Mae was on stage. She was part of the chorus at the Metropolitan Opera for years, and my cousin Audrey was so talented I just knew it was going to happen for her one day.

While many people saw working at the theater as glamorous, the truth was it was blue-collar work with long hard hours and physically demanding both on and offstage. Sewing costumes was the only trade I learned, but I learned a lot more than just costumes behind the scenes.

I knew which actresses didn't know how to hold their liquor, which ones didn't eat, and who ate too much. We always had to make alterations to their costumes. I knew who secretly loved men and who secretly loved women. I also knew who worked their way to the top and who slept their way to the top. Hollywood was not the only place where that happened. What I paid attention to the most, though, was who really had talent. I knew who the audience tuned out when they sang and who they would lean toward with rapt attention. I paid attention to what the audience responded to, so while Oscar was a paid talent scout, I had started scouting talent years before I met him.

I was lucky to have met Oscar. He married well below his potential, but I think that's what made him feel at home with me. He came from nothing and was a self-made man. Because of his upbringing, he loved to be generous to those who had less, and it was one of many traits I loved him for.

While we could afford to go to the best restaurants in New York, his favorite meal was toasted rye bread and canned peaches. It was a simple meal made of what his mother had in the house when they didn't have much. So, Friday nights, instead of going to one of our favorite restaurants, I would have peaches and rye bread waiting for him when he got home from work that we would eat on the good china with the gold rim. No one else really understood it, but it made him smile, and that made me smile.

Oscar would put on a clean suit and tie, and when I was feeling extra fashionable, I'd match his handkerchief in his lapel pocket with my dress. I knew it might have seemed over the top to some, but you could never underestimate what a first impression could make as we mingled with some of the most powerful people in the New York theater scene. Someone was always watching and judging, so if there was one thing I could control, it was that we dressed with elegance and class. We had a reputation to uphold in New York, and I did my very best to do my part in that as his wife.

Our seats were typically in the orchestra, front row center, or a few rows back. He spoiled me, and I didn't take that for granted. As soon as the playbill was in my hand, I poured over it to see if we knew anyone in the cast, who was new talent, what their bio was, and did they have representation. Oscar was busy making his rounds and came back to find me sitting in my seat with my head buried in the playbill.

He laughed and said, "Hard at work again, darling?"

"It doesn't feel like work. Is it wrong I prefer a playbill to a book?"

"Not wrong at all. So, who are we looking at tonight?"

"You know I don't like to make any preconceived judgments until at least intermission."

"What was I thinking? I will hold all questions until intermission." He kissed me on the cheek.

The lights dimmed, and I could feel the warmth of him beside me. Oscar squeezed my hand as the curtain went up, and for the next hour, I lost myself in the show. I pretended our life was full of the same passion as the lovers on stage. While everyone focused on what was happening in front of us, Oscar's hand was slowly going up my thigh. I looked at him with a scolding glance, but I saw hope in his eyes. Hope for what was and hope for what maybe could be again. I gave in to his touch, sighed, and then pulled myself together and crossed my legs. Could you imagine what people would say if they saw him touching me? I was horrified at the thought of it, and yet it was also thrilling in the moment.

The house lights came up for intermission, and Oscar turned to me and said, "What do you think?"

"The blond in the back row shouldn't have been in the back row."

"And why is that?"

"She was positively graceful. She will not be a chorus girl for long."

"Good eye, Rose. You spot potential so easily. But if I'm honest, I'm quite bored with this show. Shall we duck out before act two starts?" Suggested Oscar.

I could see the hungry look in his eyes and knew why he wanted to leave. I wished I could give him what he wanted, but I couldn't, and he knew that. Besides, it would be incredibly rude of us to just leave in the middle of the show. People would notice, and who knew what the gossip would be the next day.

"Now you know you will kick yourself if act two is better than act one, and what if there is a future star in act two just waiting for discovery? That would be a real shame to miss out on that future business opportunity."

"You are persuasive, my dear Rose. Act two it is!" he said with a smile because he knew I was right. But I saw a hint of disappointment in his eyes.

After the show, we grabbed drinks at Sardi's, and while Oscar talked shop with theater owners, agents, and producers, I was organizing the social calendar of the wives and planning dinner parties for Oscar's new clients. I did love to throw a party, and our apartment on Central Park West was typically full of actors, musicians, and industry folks from both New York, Chicago, and Los Angeles. I didn't mind it at all. It was thrilling to be at the center of everything, even if I was not the one calling the shots. I knew my job as hostess made Oscar even more successful. His success was my success, and let's face it, relationships were everything in this business. I made sure those relationships were well fed, watered, and cared for and that everyone in our company felt like a star.

We hailed a cab back uptown, and Oscar seemed a bit jittery while I was still elated from a wonderful night at the theater. We walked down our hallway headed toward our apartment, but Oscar lingered near the door of another apartment door. With keys in hand, I turned the doorknob, walked into our apartment, and changed into my robe. It was then I realized Oscar was still down the hall.

"Oscar?" I called out, wondering what on earth he was doing in the hallway.

Startled, he quickly entered our apartment and said, "Darling, did you like the show tonight?"

"You know our nights at the theater are my favorite, and I especially love when it's a musical."

"Good. You know I just want you to be happy."

"I am happy, Oscar!"

Oscar came closer to me and gently brushed the hair from my face.

Wanting to break the intimacy of the moment, I blurted out, "I'm planning on taking Audrey shopping tomorrow and then starting to get the menu ready for the Christmas party." He was not listening as he leaned in to kiss me, and I indulgently kissed him back. He started to take off my pink silk robe, and I hurriedly pulled it back on, flustered and confused. I loved him and wanted to give in to the moment, but instead, I stopped. As much as I wanted to enjoy the physical and emotional pleasure of sleeping with my husband, I just couldn't risk getting pregnant again. I could never go through the pain of losing another child, and if that meant I had to sacrifice intimacy with my husband, then that was the sacrifice I had to make. "Oscar, you know... we can't..." I whispered, knowing it was not what he wanted to hear.

And then all the hope that was in his eyes slowly deflated out of him, and he said defeated, "I know. Goodnight, my dear Rose. I'll see you at breakfast."

I walked back to the bedroom and sat down at my vanity. Oscar looked at me, sadly shook his head, and left the apartment. I didn't want to know where he was going, but I couldn't tame my curiosity. I tiptoed out of our room into the living room and put my eye through the peephole of our apartment door. I saw him walk down to the door he was lingering in front of earlier. The door opened, revealing the blond dancer from the back row in a seductive lace nightgown. She stood in her doorway, and at that moment, I thought both of us were holding our breath, wondering what would happen next.

Oscar hesitated for a split second, looked back at our apartment before he quickly kissed her and entered the apartment.

The blond welcomed his kiss and shut her door hard. I shuddered at the slam and slowly sunk down along the door, letting out a gasp. I let myself just sit on the ground for a moment as the reality of the situation sunk in.

He was cheating.

Lots of men cheat. But Oscar, Oscar was too classy to cheat, I told myself. It was so cliché, and he was not cliché. *We* were not cliché. I was in denial, and yet while I was angry and hurt by Oscar's infidelity, I was angrier with myself. I denied him something he needed. We were the couple who looked like they had everything on the outside. But no one ever knew what happened behind someone else's closed-door; or what didn't happen for that matter.

I would learn to accept this and, by looking the other way, own my part in driving him away. I took a deep breath, lifted my head up high, and walked back to the bedroom.

CHAPTER 7

WAKES AND WINE

———

AUDREY: JANE'S HOUSE, THANKSGIVING—1992

It was decades before I had learned what was happening with Rose and Oscar. I'm surprised she just shared all of that with Amelia now. These memories are bittersweet, and we are sharing our stories, so Amelia understands in some ways, as women, we were victims of the times and that often impacted our choices. She has so much more control over her life choices now than we did, and she will get to write more of her own story.

Rose has gone to get us a glass of wine, though I think she also needs a minute to collect herself. Reliving those memories couldn't have been easy. Amelia's starry eyes look a little dimmer now, and while we don't want to discourage her, we do want to share the truth of what it can mean to be a woman and the issues we might face.

"I just feel so bad for Aunt Rose," Amelia says softly.

"Oh no, don't you pity her. That's the last thing she wants," I reply.

"But Grandma, he was cheating on her!"

"Well, yes, he was, and that was wrong. But it was quite common for marriages in the 1940s to have infidelities. The wives stayed, looked the other way, and made the best of it, as painful as that was. They didn't have the same security afforded to women today. Women today can have their own careers and are empowered to walk away. And yet, their reputation and financial stability can still be at stake just like it was for women back then," I explained. "And Rose and Oscar loved each other very much, despite their situation."

"I guess I didn't think about it that way... It just seems so clear to me that when you make a commitment, you keep it," Amelia said with a small shake of her head.

"Yes, absolutely. Aunt Rose and I made several commitments, and one of them was to each other."

AUDREY: FUNERAL HOME, WINTER—1989

I know sometimes people just don't understand how integral our friends are to our own happiness. Some people don't need friends, but I needed Rose. We needed each other, both for the exciting moments of our lives and the really hard ones.

The day of my husband's wake was one such hard moment, and without her, I may not have made it through the day.

Poinsettias, red and white carnations, and holly decorated the funeral parlor for the holiday season, but Christmas decorations at a funeral just didn't seem right to me. There was nothing festive about mourning. It was a packed house, and I could barely catch my breath between the hugs and tears from family, friends, neighbors, and teachers in our community. My husband's work colleagues and friends of our family shared story after story as I smiled and nodded as graciously as I could.

I had been standing for what felt like years, surrounded by the kids, their spouses, and all my grandchildren. While I was the grieving widow, no one told me I would still have to act as the hostess at my own husband's wake. I had organized and booked the repass, paid for the funeral home, scheduled the mass, chosen the flowers, and had to hold it all together to ease everyone else's pain around me.

For me, it hadn't been the chance to say goodbye and make peace with the loss like I had hoped it would be. I hadn't even had time to process what the loss meant. My feet were aching, my head was pounding, and I really just needed to talk to my best friend and get some air.

I was talking to Peggy Taylor, one of our neighbors, going on and on about how her cat had just died and how she could understand how I was feeling. My eyes screamed over to Rose to rescue me and thank goodness she did.

"Excuse me, Audrey dear, I'm so sorry to interrupt, but Father Donahue needs to speak with you," she said, linking her arm in mine and shuffled me away from Peggy and out into the hallway.

"Thank you! I could not listen to her cat stories for one more second. How can you compare losing a cat to losing a husband?" I asked.

"You can't. Did you ever think we would both outlive our husbands?" Rose asked.

"I pictured us all growing old together," I said.

"Well, we are old, and we are together."

"And you have been there for every moment. The moments of hope, and laughter, of love, and now loss."

"I wouldn't be anywhere else." She took in my slumped shoulders, my pale face, and squirming feet and asked, "Hey, you wanna get out of here?"

"Yes, I could really use a drink."

Rose grabbed a bottle of communion wine from the parlor of the funeral home, took my hand, and we quietly snuck out to the street. We headed toward the park across the way, and instantly I felt like I could breathe again. The chill of the December air hit my face, and I could see my breath as I exhaled. Rose lit a cigarette, and a swirl of smoke wafted out, colliding with my breath in the winter air. I took a swig of the sweet communion wine, passed it to Rose, and she took a sip. We both sighed, sat down on a nearby park bench, and I leaned my head onto Rose's shoulder, padded with the soft fur of her mink coat.

"Wow. I didn't realize how much I needed some air."

"Wakes are exhausting."

"They are," I said and held up the bottle of wine as if making a toast. "Here's to the man that snuck into my heart when I wasn't looking."

I took another long swig of wine, the taste less sweet the more I drank, and passed it to Rose, who took a swig as well.

"He adored you, Audrey," Rose reminded me. "It's always a good bet to marry a man who adores you a little bit more than you adore them."

"I was so afraid of being alone then. I didn't know who I was." As soon as I said it, I realized it was true.

"And now?"

"I think I'm about to find out. I haven't been alone in over forty years. I'm scared." I really couldn't imagine what being alone would be like.

Rose took my hand in hers and said, "It would be strange if you weren't. Those first few months without Oscar were the hardest." Her words were comforting and reminded me she had been through this and survived.

"What did you do?" I asked, desperate for a solution to the pain and hoping Rose had some answers.

"I cried and prayed a lot. The one thing I couldn't bring myself to do was go to the theater without him." Rose turned her head toward me, and I saw the pain in her eyes. Their home away from home was the theater. It must have felt like a part of her had been ripped out, as her entire world revolved around Oscar and the theater.

How had she managed without the two things she loved most in the world? I knew what that felt like, and yet we still managed to keep going. While what came next for me seemed daunting and scary, that year of watching my husband die was far worse than letting him go. Oscar, may he rest in peace, had died of a heart attack. He was here one day and gone the next. My husband's death, on the other hand, was a long and slow process.

"Of course, I understand completely. He taught me how to golf one summer when the kids were little. I resisted learning, but then I actually got quite good at it. On a rare Saturday when we could, we would golf together and pretend we belonged at the fancy country club our friends would invite us to and laugh all afternoon. Now I can't even look at his clubs in the garage without breaking down."

"Oh, Audrey," Rose said, squeezing my hand.

"After the stroke, it was so hard watching him deteriorate right in front of my eyes."

I took another drink of my wine, remembering the really bad days. He needed to lean on me and his nurse for everything. He had to learn how to talk again as if reverting back to one of the many children we taught to talk and walk. He could never seem to get the words out right, and there were a lot of curse words that came out that weren't even curse words. They were a combination of what he could say and what he was trying to say. I think he invented some new words in that process.

"He's at peace now, Audrey, and he's with Oscar," Rose said quietly.

"Yes. But what about us? What do we do now?" I asked with a mix of anger and envy of our husbands. They didn't exactly leave a manual of what to do next once we were on our own.

"Well, what have you never gotten to do that you wanted to do in the last forty years?"

"You mean besides sleep?"

Rose laughed at the truth of that statement and replied, "Well, sleep first. But what about after that?"

"I don't know... travel, I guess? It just sounds so cliché." Even saying it sounds ridiculous to me. Where am I going to go by myself?

"There's nothing cliché about traveling outside of the tri-state area."

"Sure, rub it in. You know not all of us had a disposable income to leave the tristate area." I never would've said that to her twenty years ago. It's funny how age made you bolder.

"I know," she said, almost apologizing for her wealth. She paused and thought for a minute before she asked, "But if you were going to leave Jersey, where would you want to go?"

"As far away as possible?" I said jokingly.

"That's a start," Rose said encouragingly.

"You know, I was just reading this funny children's book to my granddaughter Vivienne called *Alexander and the Terrible, Horrible, No Good, Very Bad Day*. After one such bad day, he decides to move to Australia. That is definitely as far away as possible."

"Well, maybe don't *move* to Australia, but I think you might have just figured out your first trip!" Rose exclaimed with excitement.

"I guess I did! And you know what else is in Australia? The Bernstein piano competition! It's also where Wertheim pianos originated, in Melbourne."

I realized at that moment how Australia sounded more and more exciting, especially with the thought of focusing on pianos and the history of them to be found there. I've always loved pianos, their history, their making, and the different styles of pianos. It's quite fascinating.

"I don't know what any of that means, but I'm glad you're excited about it," Rose looked at me, confused with all my specific piano references, but she didn't need to know what I meant to see it was lighting me up. I began to wonder what lit her up those days.

"So... what are you excited about?"

"You're going to laugh," Rose said, giving me a look.

"I would never laugh at you, Rose," I said, dripping with sarcasm and taking her hand.

"Sure. 'Cuz you've never laughed at me before!" she said and gave me a little scolding tap on the hand.

"Oh, go on! I am intrigued."

Rose took a deep breath and started to explain, "Well, I was visiting a friend the other day at the hospital, and I walked by the maternity floor."

"I think that ship has sailed, Rose," I said dryly and then tilted my head with a smirk.

"You said you wouldn't laugh!" Rose raised her voice ever so slightly, and then I felt bad. She clearly had something on her mind, and I wasn't helping her get it out.

"I'm sorry, really. What happened at the hospital?"

"Well, there was a sign posted they are looking for volunteers to work in the nursery, and I was considering being a volunteer. Though, I'm worried they might think I'm too old or something," Rose said, and I knew this was important to her. This was a chance for her to surround herself with babies. She never had that opportunity as a young woman, and it was clearly still a source of pain for her.

"You should do it! We might be old, but we are just getting started," I said, reminding her and myself this next chapter in our lives might just be the most exciting one yet. She took my hands in hers and hugged me. I smiled, thinking how we came to the park to escape my pain, only to end up helping Rose with hers.

It had made me forget mine to help her, even if only for a few minutes.

CHAPTER 8

LEMONS

—

I remember the first time my oldest son, Robert, took a bite out of a lemon. It was his first birthday party in our backyard, and he had made his way to the drink table, where some lemon slices were next to the lemonade pitcher. He grabbed a bunch of them in his icing-covered little hand and examined them to figure out what they were.

I watched as he squeezed a slice, and the lemon juice squirted onto his cheek. Every part of me wanted to run and grab those lemons out of his hands, but I was fascinated with what he'd do next. Stubbornly, he wiped the juice off his cheek, took another slice, smelled it, and then shoved it into his mouth. He squealed with delight, and his little eyes widened as his nose scrunched up, shocked with the sudden sour sensation his tiny mouth had never had before. I scooped him up and gave him a hug.

"That's a lemon, Robbie. Lemons are both sweet and sour, just like you." I kissed him on his button nose, and then I took a sip of my ice-cold lemonade.

Robbie reached out and said, "Me try, me try, mama." I held the glass up to his mouth, and he took a big gulp and smiled wide.

There had been so much sweet mixed with sour before the children came. I wish I could go back and tell my younger self to just hold on.

AUDREY'S HOUSE: FALL—1941

There were a lot of lemons thrown at me that year.

I was home practicing some Chopin on the piano and completely at peace as my fingers effortlessly moved across the keys when Bobby came into the house fuming. He threw the first lemon of that year.

He slammed the door, waving an America First pamphlet, and then dramatically tore it up into a million pieces. I could practically see the steam coming out of him.

"Jeez, Bobby. Could you slam the door a little harder? What's wrong with you?"

"I just left a rally where Lindberg was spouting his nonsense. I could scream! People are so desperate to pretend the war is so far away and it doesn't impact us here that we don't have a duty to protect humanity and democracy in Europe. Just keep on living the American dream and ignore—"

"Bobby, stop talking about Lindberg. What are you going to do about it?" He often went to those rallies and would get all riled up. But enough was enough, and I couldn't take any more of his whining. He needed to take some sort of action. We didn't just talk about doing things in our family. We actually did them, especially when we were passionate about it.

"I'll tell you what I'm going to do about it. I'm going to enlist today, Audrey. I can make a difference and be the type of leader our military needs right now."

Oh my God. No, no, no, no. That was not what I had meant about him doing something about it! He was obviously not thinking clearly. He belonged at home, in school, as the star of the football team and a future politician. Not away at war wasting his potential. He could be a leader right here in the USA. There were lots of people who needed him to lead right here. Like me, for one.

"What? No! I was thinking maybe you just go and talk to this Lindbergh fella. You don't have to enlist!"

"I have to do something," Bobby said.

"You don't have to do anything! You can stay here with me, finish college. Why would you throw your scholarship away?"

I wondered what mom and dad would think of this. They valued our education so much and being the first generation to go to college was not something to take lightly. Our parents didn't work that hard for him to burn it all down in one rash decision to play the hero.

"I'm not throwing it away. It will still be here when I get back."

"Don't do this. Bobby, please," I pleaded, turning my full attention away from the piano to face him.

"I'll be back before you know it. Besides, you'll be so busy playing your music you won't even know I'm gone." How did he think that music was somehow going to distract me from the fact that my only brother, whom I loved more than anyone in this world, would be away at war and risking his life?

If anything, that would only distract me even more from being able to concentrate on my music.

"Of course, I will! You are my hero, Bobby. I can't lose you! I cannot and will not."

"I want to be a hero for my country." How could I talk him out of it? I saw the pride in his eyes as he spoke about wanting to be a hero, and at that moment, I knew there was no talking him out of it. Still, I had to try.

"Please, Bobby, go to your game tomorrow, don't enlist. Go win that game, win it for me. Win it for your country."

"McKenna's win!" he declared.

"And we never give up. Now promise me, don't make any decisions until after the game, for me, please, Bobby."

"Fine, Audrey. We'll talk after the game."

"Thank you! You are going to win tomorrow. I just know it!"

I gave him a huge hug and let out a sigh of relief. I didn't know how I had talked him out of that, but I was so thankful I had. Now we could just enjoy his game. I'd always loved watching Bobby play football. We all did. Rose, Oscar, Ted, Vic, and I were his official cheering section and never missed a game.

The way he took command of the field, led his teammates, made quick decisions, and ran like lightning. He was amazing. I would never have thought to describe a football player as graceful, but that was Bobby. Grace under pressure. Team over self. He was a leader at heart, and I loved him for it.

With that issue out of the way, for the time being, I had to get my dress ready for the big Carnegie audition and then practice with Vic. I was nervous but so excited. It was going to be the best day. Bobby would win his game, we'd all have fun cheering him on, and then Vic and I would go wow them at the Carnegie audition.

I just hoped Bobby would listen to reason about enlisting, but for some reason, I couldn't shake the feeling in the pit of my stomach that something was going to go wrong.

CHAPTER 9

ONE MORE GAME

AUDREY: AUDREY'S HOUSE, FALL—1941

I was running out of time. I could barely sleep the night before as my nerves were all out of sorts. The Carnegie audition was two hours after Bobby's big game, so I needed to be ready to go straight to the city with Vic immediately after. I knew I wouldn't be in football game attire, but it was never a bad thing to be the best-dressed person at an event.

Vic was coming over so we could practice for a few hours for the last time before the audition. I greeted him at the door, and his navy suit and hat looked so incredibly dapper and complimented my dress.

"You look amazing," Vic said as he took my hands and kissed me on the cheek.

"Why, thank you. So do you. *We* look amazing."

"That we do. Are you warmed up?"

"I am! Bobby wants to kill me. I've been singing all morning, but he left about an hour ago for the game, so we have the house to ourselves."

"Good, then we don't have to hold back. Why don't you go to the piano, and we'll run it a few times."

We practiced our duet four times through. My favorite part was when he sat next to me at the piano, and we played and sang together at the same time. If that wasn't impressive to the casting directors, then I didn't know what would be. Vic was oozing with charm. He lit up even brighter the second he knew he was onstage, and people were watching, but right now, there was no one watching. It was just us.

"Do you think we need to run it one more time?" I asked.

"Nope, we are cooking with gas now, Audrey! Let's take a break," Vic said.

We took a break from practicing, put a record on, and started dancing. We started to swing, and he twirled and dipped me. I was laughing and dancing so fast I was sweating and out of breath within minutes. Vic was a good dancer, much better than I was, but that's why we made such a great team.

Just as I was about to tell him we needed to slow down, a slow song came on, and he pulled me close while I closed my eyes.

He softly sang "The Way You Look Tonight" into my ear as we danced, and I pretended he was Fred Astaire and I was Ginger Rogers in Swing Time. He kissed my hair, and I could feel myself melting. I just wanted to stay there in that moment. I looked up at him and knew he could see it all over my face.

"I love you, Vic."

"I know." He smiled with that boyish grin. God, he was cocky, and I didn't care. "I love you too." He brushed the hair out of my eyes and kissed me deeply. I was completely under his spell. I didn't care what time it was or where we were supposed to be. I needed him and wanted to be there with him.

Fans in blue and white filled the Seton Hall University stadium to the brim. The crisp autumn air was cooling me down. I hurriedly rushed into the stands and found Rose, Oscar, and Ted and took a seat, thankful to catch my breath for a minute. Vic was right behind me, carrying our music for the audition. I was nervous but needed to focus on Bobby now.

I hoped he would be so motivated from winning today he wouldn't even remember wanting to enlist. How could he give all of this up? He was the star of the Football team. Football was his stage, and hopefully, with his political aspirations, he'd be on even bigger stages one day. I giggled a little to myself, thinking about how we both were performers at heart.

"Wow, you look nice," Ted said.

"Thanks, Ted. What'd we miss?" Vic asked.

"I was talking to Audrey. We're winning, up by four. "

"Hey, aren't you a little overdressed for a football game?" Rose asked.

"Our big audition is right after the game. We were busy practicing and just lost track of time."

I glanced over at Vic with a smile, and he winked at me. I could feel my cheeks flush again and hoped no one else noticed. I was suddenly incredibly self-conscious and started smoothing my hair.

"Well, you look great. Don't they look great, Oscar?" Rose said.

"Like the best-dressed couple Carnegie has ever seen," Oscar said, and then he took a bite of his hot dog. Rose handed him a napkin, taking care of him as always.

"Thank you!" I saw Bobby running on the field and screamed. "Go, Bobby!"

"Jeeze, Audrey, I can't hear," Ted said.

"Sorry, you know I get excited when Bobby's in play—oh, and I love his costume."

"It's not a costume, Audrey. It's a uniform." Ted rolled his eyes at me.

"Same thing!"

The fans were chanting "McKenna, McKenna, McKenna," and then we heard the football announcer giving the play-by-play.

"And it's third and ten and Quarterback Bobby McKenna hikes the ball, no one's open to pass to, McKenna runs outside the pocket, he's weaving through defenders, two yards to go… and McKenna and Campbell collide, Campbell head butting McKenna at full force, and McKenna tumbles, crashing head first to the ground… his neck and body twist like a pretzel on the ground… it looks, bad folks… McKenna's not getting up."

Bobby fell to the ground, but this was football. They crashed into each other all the time. They were supposed to tackle each other. Bobby trained for this, and he knew what to do. He was strong and always bounced back. I held my breath, waiting for him to get up. We were all holding our breath in the stands. You could have heard a pin drop in that stadium.

I looked at Vic with panic in my eyes, and he squeezed my hand.

"He'll be okay. Just give it a minute," he said, reassuring me.

"He just got the wind knocked out of him," Ted said,

I looked at Rose and Oscar and knew from Rose's face he had been down too long.

"Bobby!"

I screamed and started pushing through the crowd, making my way down the field. I saw him lying there still as could be. His teammates were standing around him looking like helpless little sheep, not the strong, tough men they had been just two minutes before. I crouched down on the field next to him and took his hand in mine.

"Bobby, you can't leave me! Please, Bobby, fight!"

The coach waved desperately to the medic, who rushed over. He started examining his head and neck to see where the impact was, and I saw blood and had to look away.

"He's bleeding!" I screamed at the medic, "Do something!" My heart raced, and I could barely breathe. Why was everyone moving so slowly in a moment that seemed to be happening so fast?

The medic listened to his chest and then took his pulse before looking up at me and shaking his head. I crumpled into a pile hugging Bobby's lifeless body as the tears streamed down my face. This wasn't happening. This couldn't be real. He couldn't really be gone. He was the strongest, bravest, smartest, most generous human being I knew. Men like Bobby didn't die. They lived forever.

I felt a hand on my back and looked up to find Rose, Oscar, Ted, and Vic all standing there. Rose was sheet white and looked like she might faint if it wasn't for Oscar holding her up. Ted was also visibly shaken, and Vic held his hand out to me, and I took it to steady myself as I slowly got up and fell into his arms.

We just stood there with arms around each other, crying.

Through blurry eyes, I saw a stretcher brought out to the field. They placed Bobby onto the stretcher, and his teammates lifted it up like pallbearers and carried him solemnly off the field.

That image would haunt me well into the future; brothers carrying another fallen brother off a field.

Sadly, many more brothers would be carried off many other fields in the coming years.

CHAPTER 10

BEAUTIFUL MUSIC IN FLAMES

AUDREY: AUDREY'S HOUSE, WINTER—1941

I felt empty inside. Like someone had ripped everything out and just left an empty shell. It was possible I'd never get off the couch again. I wrapped myself in a cozy blanket and shoveled warm chocolate chip cookies into my mouth, though I couldn't even taste them. Cookies could not heal the pain of losing my brother. Nothing could fill that void. Nothing could, and nothing ever would.

All I could do was pray. I looked up at the cross hanging over the fireplace, where the fire lit below was crackling merrily. I closed my eyes tightly and remembered Psalm 34:18 *'God is near to the broken hearted and saves those who are crushed in spirit.'*

"Lord, hear my prayer," I whispered, though silence was my only answer. It was broken by the sound of the door creaking, and I opened my eyes. Vic was there, and I smiled, hoping he would comfort me. My eyes adjusted, blurry from the tears I'd been crying, and I realized what I was actually looking at.

Were my eyes playing tricks on me? Vic was standing before me in an army uniform. My eyes scanned his four-pocket, drab olive coat, and matching trousers. His cap rested slightly to the left of his thick dark hair, and the gold buttons on his coat shined back at me as if someone had just polished them.

It was not a costume.

He was standing taller than usual, and his shoulders looked broad and strong. In one hand, he was holding a big army duffel bag, and in another hand, his guitar case. He slowly approached me, and I could barely get the words out.

"What have you done?" I said as I pushed the plate of cookies onto the coffee table and held onto the couch, steadying myself as I stood, the blanket falling to the floor.

He had betrayed me. He had betrayed our love, our plans, our dreams. I felt like a lovesick fool. I stood there helplessly, waiting for an explanation.

"I have a duty to my country. Just listen for a minute—" he said as he walked closer to me.

"I thought you had a duty to me."

"I have to fight."

He didn't have to fight. He was choosing to. He had enlisted on his own. No one made him do it. He chose to honor his country over honoring me. Some people might have found that admirable, brave even, but not now. This wasn't brave. It was cowardice. He was clearly running away from me, from our dreams, from our love, from our music. I walked over to the piano and gingerly placed my fingers on the keys.

"What about our music?" I said, looking down at the keys. He walked over to the piano and sat down on the bench next to me and placed his fingers on top of mine.

"We have the rest of our lives to make music," he said, like the threat of dying in the war hadn't crossed his mind. What if we didn't have the rest of our lives? What if him walking out the door was him walking to his own death? There would be no music after that.

I looked at him with sadness, yet his bright amber eyes filled with love and hope. His eyes brought me back to that day on the beach. We were full of joy and bursting with love as he swirled me around, my dress twirling in the summer breeze like they did in the movies. Life without music, life without each other, was simply gray. Did he even mean any of what he had said then? I doubted myself and him. Maybe if I reminded him of that moment, he'd change his mind.

"The whole world is waiting for us," I said his words back to him, inching closer to him on the bench.

"Our country needs me."

"I need you!" I said and reached for his hands." I can't audition without you. We're a duo act."

He dropped my hands, stood up, and said, "The audition? That's all you can think of right now? How selfish can you—"

"Selfish? *I'm* selfish?" I cut him off. "You're the one breaking promises," I said as I got up from the piano.

"I'm the one serving my country. Audition without me. What do I care?" he said as he walked to the fireplace and threw a piece of music into the fire. I watched in shock and pain as the music blazed, the notes fading away into the flames.

I'd pushed him too far. He was yelling now, and so was I. I had to get him to see reason and to see what he was giving up. The truth was I couldn't audition without him. Our act was us. It wasn't about me. It was the chemistry we had together, both on stage and off, as he had said. Audiences wanted to see couples in love.

I didn't think I *could* do it without him. It would just be a reminder of his absence.

"I don't want to do anything without you." I walked closer to him, feeling the warmth of the fire and him, and reached for his hand. He laced his fingers with mine and started to soften.

"You can do anything, Audrey. By the time I come back, you'll be the greatest act Carnegie has ever seen!" He wasn't hearing me! I ripped my hands apart from his and started pacing. I didn't even recognize the sounds coming out of my mouth. They were desperate, angry, and powerful.

"Vic, it's not about Carnegie! How can you leave after Bobby just died? What if you don't come back?"

"I'll come back."

He seemed so sure, but did he know how difficult waiting for the man I loved, going off to war, would be for me?

"I thought we'd be getting married soon… and now…" What if—I tried to ignore the thought.

"I can't even think about marriage right now Audrey, I need to fight for our country and Bobby."

Crushed, I ran to him and said desperately, "I need you," into his chest.

"I need you too. It's going to be okay, I promise," he said and pulled me into him. We stood there for a moment, clinging to each other. I was trying to memorize every inch of his face. The dimples in his cheeks when he smiled, the way his thick eyebrows furrowed when he was thinking, his knowing smile that made me want to jump into his arms and kiss him until I couldn't breathe.

"When do you leave?"

"I ship out tomorrow."

"Tomorrow?"

I heard someone clearing their throat and turned my gaze in the direction of the sound, noticing Ted standing near the door. He walked toward us, and I had to wonder when he had arrived. Had he been there that whole time? I inched a step away from Vic and noticed Ted was in uniform too. So, they had done this together. They both went behind my back and decided without me. Did women ever get a say in these things?

"Ted! Not you too!"

"Yes, but I got a different assignment. I'm assigned to Brooklyn Yard to teach the soldiers how to read. Not exactly what I signed up for."

Ted was minimizing his smarts. He had a teaching degree and should've been proud the army valued his brains over his strength. Anyone could fight, and these men all had something to prove. I hoped they were not trying to prove something to me. I'd much rather they all just stayed right there, safe and sound, with everything staying the same, filling our days and nights with fun, not worrying about the realities of war.

"I think that's a very important job, and Brooklyn, well, that's not very far at all!" I replied.

"No, it's not." He looked down at his shoes, avoiding our gazes. "I can look out for you while Vic's gone."

"I don't need looking out for," I said.

"You don't, but with your brother gone, I'm thankful Ted *is* here in case you did... need something," Vic said and pulled me toward him. "But God will be faithful. I will come back to you."

"From your lips to God's ears," I said as I crossed myself and kissed the gold cross around my neck. I took the necklace off slowly and placed it in Vic's hands.

"Here. To remember me when your faith is tested." He took the necklace from my hands as his eyes locked with mine. The reality that this could be our last moment together sunk in.

"I don't want you to go," I said softly. "Doesn't the army know how much I need you? I'm scared, Vic."

"And I don't want to leave you…" He kissed me slowly, both of us wanting to savor the moment and make it last as long as possible.

I refused to believe that would be the last time I would see him, hear his voice, or feel his lips on mine. He wrapped me in his arms, and I buried my head in his chest. We held onto each other, desperate not to let go. He sang to me as only he could.

Beautiful Music Together

VIC
Every day I'll wait for your letters
I'll cling to them to fill my dreams
Of you and I together
melody and harmony
And when I close my eyes
And I'll start dreaming
I'll hear you
And your music will keep me alive
I'll see you
and your smile will keep me from drowning
I'll feel you
and I'll pray for the day
I'll hold you again
and we'll make beautiful music together

He wouldn't admit he was scared, but I could feel his heart beating so quickly against his chest, and his hands were trembling. He pulled himself away, and we looked at each other in silence. I was searching in his eyes for another answer. I could barely breathe.

'Change your mind!'

"We better go, Vic," Ted said.

'Ask me to marry you!'

"Yeah."

'Please don't leave me here like this, alone.'

He grabbed my hands and pulled me into him, and we clung to each other one last time. He closed his eyes and kissed me softly, and I felt his eyelashes wet with tears against my cheeks. He started to pull away, and I held onto the couch to steady my knees that were shaking beneath me.

"Goodbye, Audrey," Vic said softly. He picked up his big army duffel bag, grabbed his guitar case, and walked out the door.

That was not the answer I had been looking for.

ACT 2

CHAPTER 11

HOPE AND GRACE

ROSE: JANE'S HOUSE, THANKSGIVING—1992

"It was hard to watch your grandmother lose so much all at once," I say to Amelia as I squeeze Audrey's hand." Watching her heart break over and over, I don't think I'll ever forgive Vic for leaving her at that moment, as patriotic as his choice was."

"How could he leave after your brother just died?" Amelia asked curiously.

"Only Vic knows the answer to that," Audrey answered.

"But losing Bobby, so young and full of life, and in such a tragic and unexpected way rocked all of us to the core. But isn't that what people always say about death? It's the ultimate interrupter."

"That it is," Audrey agrees, her eyes filled with pain.

"I knew how your grandmother felt, having suffered my own unexpected loss. I carried that burden of grief on my own for many, many years."

ROSE: ROSE AND OSCAR'S APARTMENT, FALL—1938

Oscar and I always thought we would have children one day. After enjoying the freedom of our first year of marriage, we decided we would just let nature take its course and see what happened. No pressure, just enjoy each other and pray when God wanted us to be parents, we would be.

Oscar was such a romantic in those early years of marriage. He always had a love and gift for the piano, and many nights when he would come from work, I'd pour him a drink, and he would play Gershwin or Cole Porter, and I'd sit next to him on the piano bench and sing along. Those years before his success took off in the theater world were some of my favorites—just the two of us in the apartment and all his attention on me.

I loved our freedom, our nights out in the city seeing shows, going to the movies, dinners at expensive restaurants, and Saturday afternoon walks through Central Park. Oscar loved to sleep in, and I'd have to wake him up to grab coffee and croissants at our favorite corner bakery and walk and talk while taking in the beauty of the city.

Our lives went on like this for another year until one month, nothing felt right. I could barely get out of bed in the morning, the smell and texture of chicken made me gag, and all I wanted to eat every day was potato chips, Chinese food, and ice cream, salty and sweet. I needed a combination of both and couldn't get enough. One night at dinner, Oscar took notice.

"Rose, are you feeling all right?"

"Yes, why do you ask?"

"Well, you've always been such a light eater. I don't think I've ever seen you with such a hearty appetite before."

"Oh, dear, that is embarrassing. I hope you don't think I'm overeating."

"No! Not at all. It's nice to see you enjoying your food."

I'd always been a very light eater, so this sudden change in appetite was astounding to me and embarrassing for Oscar to make mention of without any context as to why. But I didn't dare hope what that meant, and I didn't want to tell Oscar until I knew for sure. I scheduled an appointment with my doctor that week and waited for the results.

I remember that morning so vividly.

I was wearing my pink polka dot robe and matching slippers, my hair was still up in rollers from the night before, and I had just poured myself a cup of tea to settle my stomach. The phone rang, and I jumped out of my seat to get it.

I couldn't believe the words coming out of the doctor's mouth "Congratulations, Mrs. Wagner, you are pregnant!" Oscar was in the shower, so he hadn't heard the phone ring. When he came out, I was just standing next to the phone, still holding the receiver. I'd forgotten to hang up.

"What is it?" he asked me curiously. I was still in shock, but the concerned look on Oscar's face brought me back to reality. This was good news! No need for him to be concerned.

"We're having a baby!" I said excitedly.

"What? Are you sure?"

"Yes, that was the doctor calling to confirm."

"Oh, Rose! You just made me the happiest man alive!" Oscar ran to me, kissing me as he put his hand on my stomach gently. He then knelt down to talk to my belly. "I can't wait to meet you. You are going to be the most interesting little guy on ninety-third street."

"Or little girl!" I added, giving him a big smile.

"Yes, or little girl. I'm calling in sick today. We need to celebrate."

"Oh, Oscar, are you sure? We can celebrate tonight."

"No, no, we need to remember this day. Go get dressed. I'm taking you out."

We spent the entire day together. It was a gorgeous sunny day in October and seasonably warmer than usual. We walked down to Riverside Park and out on a pier to look out at the water, so hopeful of the future. We held hands like a couple of young sweethearts and took in the sun glimmering off the water. Oscar wrapped his arms around me, and we just stood there in silence for a few minutes, deep in our thoughts.

"I wonder if he'll look like you or me?" he said.

"I don't know. I guess we'll have to wait and see what *he or she* could look like."

We walked along the pier and stopped for lunch at a nearby café overlooking the water. The sky was as blue as a robin's egg with barely any clouds to be found, and the sun felt warm and cheerful on my cheeks. Birds were chirping, and a lovely autumnal breeze was blowing. I happily licked my strawberry ice cream as the clouds started moving in, shading the sun.

A couple of months later, we received an invitation to a party at our friend's apartment. I was excited to show off my growing baby bump to the other mothers at the party. You could only be a married couple without children for so long without the vultures swarming in and asking all sorts of questions that were none of their business. Well, that night, I walked in proudly wrapped in my fur coat and blush pink dress that showed just enough to be obvious I didn't just eat too much strawberry ice cream. As soon as I handed my coat to our hostess, Gloria, her eyes scanned my dress and landed right on my belly, and then the rest of the women came flocking over.

I didn't mind the attention. It was my time, and I was happy to quiet the rumors Oscar and I didn't want children. Then the advice started and didn't seem to stop for the entire night.

"Well, when my Billy was born, I told Walter, we must have a wet nurse. You can't expect me to stay up all night with him, can you?"

"Right, of course. With my Betty, all I could eat was peanut butter by the spoonful. We really should've just named her peanut." The women all started cackling away, and I could barely get a word in edgewise.

"You know, you should think about getting one of those new carriages from that new baby boutique around the corner. They are all the rage."

"Now the best hospital is, of course…"

It went on and on like this for a good hour. I was sipping ginger ale, trying to tune the unwanted advice out of my head, when I felt a horrible cramp in my side. It felt like a painful menstrual cramp. I winced but managed to make my way to the powder room quickly. When I looked down at my underwear, I saw it was covered in blood. Not pink spotting like I'd had before. This was deep, red blood that had soaked right through my underwear and had started to drip down my leg.

I felt faint and had to hold onto the side of the wall not to fall over. The cramps were getting so much stronger I needed to clench my teeth and fists through the pain. I knew this was bad, but I refused to think the worst. I couldn't. I had to get out of that bathroom and to Oscar without causing a scene. I realized that would be difficult as the blood just kept coming, and the pain was getting worse. In the linen closet, I found a large towel and wrapped it around my now ruined dress. I grabbed two smaller hand towels and placed them in my underwear, trying to soak up the blood.

I splashed water on my face and opened the door, terrified of what I had to do next. As I opened the door, Gloria's housekeeper, Ethel, greeted me, and I grabbed her and pulled her back into the bathroom with me.

"Ethel. I have a medical emergency. I need you to find Oscar, get our coats, and apologize to Gloria and Stan. Tell them I cut myself by accident on my glass. I'm so sorry for all the blood in here. I don't want to alarm you."

"Yes, Mrs. Wagner, right away. I'll call you a taxi too."

"Thank you. And I would so appreciate your discretion in this matter. I don't want to ruin a lovely evening for everyone here."

"I understand. I will go get Oscar right away."

That one minute waiting for Oscar felt like an eternity. His face was panic-stricken when he saw my state and the towel wrapped around me covered in blood. He carefully placed my fur coat around my shoulders and put his arms around me, walking me out as quickly and as gently as he could. We didn't speak until we got into the cab, and then the tears exploded out of me.

"New York-Presbyterian Hospital, as fast as you can," Oscar said to the cabby.

"Oh, Oscar. I don't understand why this is happening! What did I do wrong?"

"Now, darling, you didn't do anything wrong. Not one thing. Just breathe. It's going to be ok. I'm here, and I love you."

"But Oscar, what if—" I could hardly form sentences around the tears pouring down my face and trying to catch my breath. "What if… we lose… if we lose…"

"No more talking. It's going to be all right," Oscar comforted me.

We made it to the hospital in record time and finally got settled into a room where a doctor could examine me. They made Oscar wait outside. I was still bleeding heavily and was in so much pain I couldn't stop crying, so they gave me a sedative. Before dozing off, the last thing I remembered was feeling like something was coming out of me, but I didn't dare look. When I woke up from my groggy haze, I heard the words that would change my life forever.

"I'm so sorry," the doctor said.

"Why? Why are you sorry?" I asked.

"For your loss."

"What loss?" My head was pounding, and my whole body ached in places it had never ached before. I didn't know what the doctor was talking about, and I just wanted to go back to sleep.

"Rose, I think what the doctor is trying to say is…" Oscar said.

"No! Don't, Oscar. I need to hear *him* say it." The pounding in my head grew louder, and my hands started shaking as my patience with Oscar and the doctor waned.

"The baby didn't make it."

"No, no, you're wrong! You have to be wrong!" It felt like a whole marching band was pounding on a drum in my head, the heat was rising in my body, and the taste of bile was coming up the back of my throat.

"Rose, it's all right. It's going to be okay." Oscar reached for my hand, and I slapped it away. I didn't want coddling. I wanted my baby back.

"It is *not* going to be okay!" I screamed. I couldn't breathe, I couldn't see straight, I don't even think I had heard him correctly. At that moment, every dream, every hope of being a mother left me.

"I know it seems that way right now, but you are young and healthy. I'm sure you will conceive again."

"Yes, we will," Oscar said and kissed me on the forehead, trying so hard to comfort me. I looked up at the doctor and Oscar in disbelief but still needed to know one more thing. I needed to know what I was too afraid to look at.

"Doctor, were you able to see the sex?"

"Yes, it was a girl." A girl. A beautiful little girl who I would never get to meet.

I would have named her Grace.

I saw Grace's whole life flash before my eyes, who she would've been, the daughter I only knew in my heart for a few short months. I would never get to rock her to sleep, brush her hair, watch her take her first steps, bring her to the theater, take her to ballet class and piano lessons, and watch her grow up into a young woman. I wouldn't get to send her off to an Ivy League college or go wedding dress shopping with her and throw her a big New York City wedding. I wouldn't get to hold my grandchild one day when she became a mother. I wouldn't get to do any of those things because they were robbed from me.

How could God have let it happen? How could you ever explain the loss of a child?

I felt empty and dead inside. Conceiving again was inconceivable to me. I would never, ever, go through this again, no matter what it cost me.

CHAPTER 12

FRIENDS WITH SECRETS

AUDREY: BOBBY'S GRAVE, WINTER—1942

I needed to talk to Bobby. I know it might have sounded silly since he wasn't really there. I knew that logically and spiritually, but I just missed my brother. I missed his tact and how he could cheer me up, calm me down, or fire me up, all in one conversation. That's what we did for each other.

There was so much more I wanted to say to him, and I thought back to our conversation before the game and talking him out of enlisting. What if he had enlisted before the game? What if he'd missed that last game because he was enlisting? He'd still be here. It was all my fault. I talked him out of it.

As I walked up to his grave, the words just started pouring out of me, as if he really could hear me.

"I'm so sorry, Bobby. I hope you can forgive me. Your death was just the beginning. Vic and I were listening to the radio, and a news broadcast announced the tragic attack on Pearl Harbor and America was going to War." I paused and wiped away a few tears. "You were right, war was coming, and when it did, Vic enlisted. He didn't have to, but he did… just like I know you wanted to."

I paused, staring at his gravestone as I tried to process the feelings that were once more overwhelming me. Feelings I'd been having since the day I had lost Bobby. "I don't think I'm ever going to recover from losing you, Bobby. Everyone I love just keeps leaving me. These strong, beautiful men, one after the other. It's just too much loss to bear."

More than a Brother

AUDREY
You were more than a brother
Unlike any other I've ever known
our family cornerstone
How can I go on
When my guidepost is gone?

We used to walk through the park on the way home
Dreaming of who we would marry one day
He used to say, "Oh Audrey, You're so witty"
And I'd say "Bobby, You'll be King one Day"

Nothing can stop the McKenna's
We make a goal get out of our way
But something stopped this McKenna
The day God took my Bobby away

I heard feet shuffling and realized I wasn't alone anymore. I was about to be caught singing and talking to a dead person like it was normal—though maybe it was. Grief could make you do crazy things. I turned my head to see Ted coming to a stop beside me, his face solemn.

"Ted, I didn't hear you walk up. What are you doing here?"

"I'm sorry, I didn't mean to startle you. I'd say I'm here for the same reason you are… to talk to Bobby." Ted slowly knelt and put flowers on Bobby's grave, and I knew he was hurting too. We both had lost our best friend.

"He always was the best listener, wasn't he?"

"Yeah."

"He would've made an amazing public speaker. That charisma he had… he drew people in." I could picture him in the future, the future he'd never have, shaking hands and kissing babies. He had the face and energy of a politician. Warm, handsome, strong, humble, and charming, all at the same time.

"I could tell him anything," Ted replied.

"Me too. He had a way of making you feel like the most important person in the room, and he always made me laugh. Remember that night with the Teddy bear?"

"How could I forget it? That bear was my date for the night," Ted chuckled.

"That was such a fun summer. The gang was all together. I miss them so much."

"I do too," Ted said softly.

Thinking of us all together again felt like another punch in the gut. Everything had been in front of us then; hopes, dreams, and love. The tears were coming again, and though I really didn't want to cry in front of Ted, I couldn't help it. They just wouldn't stop. Ted put his arms out to embrace me, and we just stood there for a moment. I was exhausted. The loss of Bobby was gnawing away at me, and then the person I was used to leaning on, Vic, wasn't there either. That hole just added to the pain, and I was so lonely.

These lemons in life were just too much. I needed some lemonade in the middle of so much loss.

Everything felt heavy like I could barely hold my head up. I put my head on Ted's shoulder for a minute and closed my eyes. When I lifted my head back up, he wiped a tear from my face ever so gently and looked at me with both sadness and yearning. I could almost hear his eyes say, '*I want to protect you.*' There was an unspoken understanding of each other's pain said in the silence between us, but he must have mistaken my pain for something else as he leaned in and kissed me softly.

It felt wrong.

It was all wrong and very confusing. What would Vic think if he saw Ted kissing me? What would Bobby think? There would be punches thrown, that much I knew for sure. I pulled away with an image of Vic pummeling Ted in my head.

"I should go," I said quickly, stepping back from Ted.

"I'm sorry, I... I didn't—" Ted stammered awkwardly.

"It's okay. I just need to go." I walked away briskly, and only once I had put some distance between us did I turn back slowly to look at him. Ted was pacing and mumbling angrily to himself, and suddenly I felt a little guilty.

I hadn't meant to hurt him or lead him on. Had I done something to give him that impression? He'd been kind, and I... I cared about Ted. He was practically family, but between losing Bobby and Vic leaving, my brain and heart were just about ready to burst. I didn't want to worry about Ted too. It was nice having him there to listen to me and console me, and *hold* me...

No, no! I did not want to have that thought. He was my friend, and he was going to stay my friend. I hoped this wouldn't make things strange between us now because I couldn't afford to lose anyone else.

ROSE: ROSE AND OSCAR'S APARTMENT, LATER THAT NIGHT—1942

"Rose! Oscar! Are you home?"

I got out of bed groggily and walked into Oscar's room to see if he heard the banging and the yelling at the door.

I turned on the light to his room and saw his bed was empty. I had thought he might be home, but I guess he'd gone out after saying goodnight.

I put on my robe and headed to the door as I heard more banging. Goodness gracious, what on earth was happening out there?

"Hey! Rose, Oscar, Open up! It's me, Ted!" It sounded like Ted, but not really. I looked into the peep hole to confirm. It was Ted, but he was slurring his speech, and he sounded more gravelly than usual. Still, I was glad I had checked. It was very late, and I was home alone.

I needed to be careful. He looked like a disheveled mess, and the neighbors in our building were so nosy. It was one thing for Oscar to be out late or stroll in the next morning, but for someone to see me letting a very drunk and loud young soldier into our apartment at night was another thing all together. We were lucky our doorman, Louie, was always discreet, respectful, and protective of our privacy.

The gossip that spread in the world of the Upper West Side of Manhattan could be brutal. I opened the door, and Ted stumbled in. He was slurring his words and could barely stand.

"It's two o'clock in the morning. What are you doing here?" I asked.

"Is Oscar here? I could use a—a whisky."

"He's not home." I hoped he wouldn't ask why because I was in no mood to explain. Besides, it seemed Ted had much bigger issues than I did. He fumbled over to the bar cart, tripping on his own two feet, and managed to quickly find the whisky, pouring himself a drink.

I grabbed the glass out of his hand. "You smell like you've already had enough whisky to last you a lifetime. What you need is a strong cup of coffee." I walked him over to the couch and away from the bar. "Here, lay down, and I'll go make you a fresh pot of coffee. Are you hungry?"

"I could eat," he said with a hiccup and sunk into the couch.

"I'll be right back... and stay away from the bar cart, please." I was suddenly very awake and headed to the kitchen to put the coffee on. I put two slices of white bread in the toaster and scrambled up some eggs with cheddar cheese while the coffee was brewing. He needed something to soak up all that alcohol.

When the eggs and toast were ready, I poured him a big glass of water and got two aspirin out of the medicine cabinet. His head was going to hurt something awful tomorrow. He liked his beer and a good Irish Whisky, but he didn't get falling down drunk like that. I wondered what had happened. I placed the food, coffee, and water with aspirin on a serving tray and walked out to the living room.

"Here we go, drink the water and aspirin first, then let's..." I stopped short when I found Ted punching the couch pillows. "Ted! Stop! What are you doing? What happened?"

"I kissed Audrey." Oh, my goodness, I needed to sit down. I was suddenly dying to know how Audrey had responded to this. Knowing Audrey, she must have had a strong reaction to Ted kissing her. The question, however, was if it was a positive or negative reaction. I knew how heartbroken and lonely she had been, and I wondered if I should encourage Ted or discourage him? Had he kissed her in a weak moment? I hoped he wasn't drunk when he had. I needed to hear more of the story.

"Oh, well, did she kiss you back?" I ventured tentatively.

"Kinda—sorta… I don't know," he sighed out.

"How do you kinda, sorta kiss someone?"

"She stopped it."

I quirked a brow. "What do you mean she stopped it?"

"She pulled away."

"What did she say after?"

"That she had to go. Ugh, I'm such an idiot!" he moaned sadly.

My Time

TED

Good job Ted
Messed it up again
She doesn't want you
She's still in love with him

I could walk away
I could stay the loyal friend
If he comes home
She'll never choose
the safe guy in the end

When's it gonna be my time?
When's it gonna be time for me to win?
When's it gonna be my time?
No more taking it on the chin

ROSE
Remember she's grieving
That's not about you
She needs to heal
Time will tell what to do

TED
I'll be strong

ROSE
If she falls apart

TED
I'll be funny

ROSE
Funny with heart

TED
I'll be the friend
turned hero

ROSE
It's a start!
He might be fire
But you can be earth
Roots firmly planted
With water, there's birth

TED
It's gonna be my time
It's time for me to win

It's gonna be my time
and I will show to everyone
That a good guy like me can win!

Listening to Ted, I pitied him. It was so clear he needed to win at something. He was deflated but starting to get some wind back in his sails. He needed a friend just as much as Audrey did, and I could be that friend to both of them. He just needed some encouragement and someone to listen and root for him.

"Of course, a good guy can win. You are a gem, Ted. She'd be lucky to have you."

"She'll never love me like the way she loves Vic." I thought he was right about that, but I would not bruise his already fragile ego and drunken state.

He kept swaying side to side on the couch like a wobbly metronome. Who was I to judge what could happen? Audrey was crazy about Vic, and I mean crazy. Those two were like electricity together, but I could see a different kind of love with Ted for Audrey. It would be softer. Maybe not as much passion, but I think she could love him if she were able to let go of Vic.

"You don't know unless you try," I encouraged him.

"Well, I kinda already did, and look at how that turned out!"

"Timing is everything. She's not ready, so you need to be patient and kind. Be her friend."

"She already has you."

"She needs all the friends she can get right now, Ted. She's grieving. She's lonely, and she needs people around her who love her and want what's best for her."

"You think I'm what's best for her?"

"I don't know what's best for her. Only her heart knows that. But it's clear you love her."

"I always have."

"I know."

"Do you think other people know?"

"Only to those of us who were paying attention."

"So, what do I do now?"

"Drink your coffee, eat your eggs and toast, and I'll call you a cab. I don't know what Oscar would think if he came home and found a drunk Ted on our couch."

"It wouldn't be much different than all of your theater party nights, now, would it?"

"I guess not, but still, I think you need to go home and sleep this off."

"Yeah, Okay. Thanks for listening—and for breakfast."

"Anytime, Ted. Anytime. Just next time, not at two in the morning, all right?"

"You got yourself a deal."

After we both had some very early breakfast, I called him a cab and got him to the elevator. The coffee, water, and food seemed to have sobered him up, and I was happy I could help. I walked back to my apartment and sat down on the couch and finished the rest of my own coffee. There was no point in trying to go back to bed now. I had too much on my mind.

What had I gotten myself into? Whose side of this love triangle was I on? I couldn't tell Audrey that Ted had come here. I would be betraying Ted's trust, and if I told her I encouraged him, well, that would sound like I was betraying both Audrey and Vic's trust.

How could I help both of them without it being too obvious? I sat there thinking and worrying and then picked up a book and started to read to distract myself and pass the time when an idea came to me. I would give Ted the fourth ticket meant for Vic to see *Lady in the Dark* with Oscar, Audrey, and me. It wouldn't be a date, just four friends out at the theater for a night. I was quite pleased with my idea when I heard the door creek open slowly, and I knew it was Oscar returning and trying not to wake me; too late. I'd been up for hours.

"Rose? What are you doing up?" He sounded both surprised and confused to find me up.

"I could say the same for you, darling." It came out a bit more quipped than I intended, but that didn't seem to faze him.

"Late night at the theater," he replied quickly.

"Right, of course."

"What's with all of the dishes?" I hadn't bothered cleaning up after Ted left, so the evidence of his visit was in plain view.

"Oh, I just had a little late-night snack. I was craving scrambled eggs and toast," I quickly explained.

"That's not like you. You never eat late at night."

"I couldn't sleep," I replied with a shrug.

"Everything okay?"

"Everything's fine. Why don't you go rest, and I'll make some more eggs if you're hungry."

"All right, thanks, dear. Eggs sound great." He went to his room, and I washed the dishes and made breakfast again. It felt good to have my own secret. Oscar certainly had plenty of his own.

But his weren't really secrets because I already knew.

CHAPTER 13

LAUGHTER IS A WONDERFUL SOUND

AUDREY: THEATER DISTRICT OF NEW YORK, SPRING—1942

Sometimes the only thing that can stop you from crying is laughing with your friends. The loss of Bobby, and Vic leaving, weighed me down, and I didn't think I had any tears left. It was after the bombing of Pearl Harbor, and our country was at War. The world felt heavy and dark, like a weighted blanket of sorrow covered it, and we all needed some light.

The twinkling lights of the Broadway marquees flashed in my eyes, reminding me the city was very much alive even at such a trying time in our country and in my heart. There was something about the energy of the Theater District that was contagious like you could almost taste the ambition in the air. A waft of roasted peanuts from a street vendor hit my nose, and I could feel my senses starting to wake up. I had forgotten how to feel anything other than pain.

Rose and Oscar were doing their best to remind me tonight. Oscar had gotten tickets for us to see *Lady in the Dark*, a musical Rose, and I had been hoping to see for a while. Rose had invited Ted to come out with us since he was currently on leave from the army and stationed right in Brooklyn. I hadn't seen him since he... since *we* had kissed. I hadn't told Rose about the kiss because I had tried really hard to pretend it hadn't happened. But it had. I was so confused and hurting, but I couldn't stop thinking about the way he had looked at me right *before* he kissed me. Something in his eyes said, *'I want to protect you if you'll let me,'* and I believed him.

I was nervous about how the night would go after Rose had told me he was coming. I hoped seeing the show would keep the talking or any awkwardness to a minimum.

"So glad you could join us, Ted! You look very handsome tonight," Rose said and then looked right at me. Ted was in his olive-green wool uniform, and as much as I didn't want to notice, he *did* look handsome. I was in a deep burgundy wine dress with a black hat and black heels with bows on them, and Rose, dressed to the nines in her usual blush pink dress, gloves, and matching hat. Even her shoes were pink with silver buckles, a favorite embellishment. On her arm was Oscar, also smartly dressed in a dapper navy suit with a matching fedora hat.

"Well, thanks, Rose, you look swell yourself. And a night out on the town with friends was something I couldn't resist," Ted replied, giving Rose an awkward smile. I wondered what that was about. "Besides, I'm under strict orders from the United States Army to cheer up Audrey."

"Nobody orders me around, Ted. You know that," I said.

"This is coming straight from Uncle Sam himself," Ted said with a big grin and a salute like he was on a mission to make me laugh. He managed to make me smile a bit.

Rose, Oscar, and Ted sang to me outside the theater with the commitment of a movie musical like *Holiday Inn*. The three of them were dancing to the swing beat of the music, and I couldn't help but tap my feet along with them.

Laughter Is a Wonderful Sound

OSCAR/ROSE
When your heart is heavy
and your tears keep weighin' you down
don't forget that laughter
is a wonderful sound
oh, laughter is a wonderful sound

OSCAR/ ROSE/ TED
Ha Ha Ha Ha Ha
Ha Ha Ha Ha Ha Ha Ha Ha

TED/OSCAR
Don't worry about tomorrow
When we're alive today

ROSE
The boys over there are fighting
Let's hear it for the USA!

TED/OSCAR
So, stop being blue
We've got an important job to do
We want to make you laugh

Ted and Oscar acted out this ridiculous bit pretending to be Abbot and Costello, and I recognized what they were trying to do with their voices right away. Their comedy radio program *The Abbott and Costello show* was a major hit, and they were two of the most popular comedians in the world right now. Their comedy provided the break we all needed from reality. Ted squeaked out this childish high-pitched-sounding voice just like Costello, and Oscar played the straight man, Abbot.

Oscar started, "How old is your baby brother?"

Ted bantered back, "About a year old,"

"Huh! I've got a dog a year old, and he can walk lots faster than the kid can," Oscar said.

"He ought to," was the reply. "He's got twice as many legs!" Ted finished the bit while Rose and I smiled ear to ear.

"You two are ridiculous!" I said.

"Yeah, but you love it," Oscar said as he smiled at Rose.

"Should we warn Abbot and Costello there's a new comedy duo in town?" Rose asked.

"You bet—let's finish this thing, Oscar," Ted said and put his arm around Oscar.

"Come on, Audrey, let's show them how it's really done."

TED/OSCAR
When your heart is heavy

ROSE/AUDREY
When your heart is heavy

TED/OSCAR
And your tears keep weighing you down

ROSE/ AUDREY
And your tears keep weighing you down
Don't forget that laughter

ROSE/AUDREY
Don't forget that laughter

TED/OSCAR
Is a wonderful

ROSE/AUDREY
Is a wonderful sound

ROSE, AUDREY, OSCAR, TED
Oh laughter, is a wonderful Sound
Ha Ha Ha Ha Ha
Ha Ha Ha Ha Ha Ha Ha Ha
Ha Ha Ha Ha Ha Ha Ha Ha

"Come on, Audrey, let's go see what Broadway has to offer us tonight," Ted urged.

Rose grabbed my hand, and the four of us walked into the theater, where we enjoyed two hours of escape from the real world. I immediately could empathize with the main character Liza's struggles with both love and life. The dialogue was witty, and the lyrics were woven intelligently in and out of gorgeous melodies that were both haunting and upbeat.

Watching the performers sing their hearts out, connecting the emotion to each lyric and phrase, filled me with so much joy and adoration for their talent. I couldn't help but close my eyes and imagine myself up on the stage. The dance numbers and costumes sparkled and then the lead actor, Danny Kaye, rattled off the most impressive patter song, naming Russian composer after Russian composer that had me laughing so hard my side hurt.

"Oh, my goodness, I can't remember the last time I laughed like that! Thank you, Oscar!" I said as we walked out of the theater.

"Anything for family!" Oscar said.

"Danny Kaye was hysterical," Ted pointed out.

"He sure was," I said, feeling lighter than I had in months.

Rose turned to Oscar and gently touched his arm. "He's someone for you to call for a meeting, Oscar. His comic timing was genius. Maybe you can steal him from his current agent," she offered, and Oscar nodded in agreement.

Ted looked to me and said, "What's that saying? Laughter is the best medicine?"

"Well, it was just the right dose for me tonight. Seeing this show made me realize how much I miss performing," I replied.

"Well, what are you waiting for?" Rose asked.

"I'm a bit rusty. I haven't performed since—"

"You're a girl. You're Irish. You can do anything!" Rose cut me off.

"I know. You never seem to let me forget that!" I replied with a smile.

"Audrey, I can make some calls. If you are serious, I can get you into some auditions this week. I can't make any promises, but I can at least get you in the door. You'll have to do the rest," Oscar said.

Picturing the actors on stage that night, I wondered who opened doors for them. I knew this business was not for the faint of heart. Some aspiring performers might think getting a little help from their friends was cheating. They wanted to make it on their own merit and talent. I wanted the same, but I was grateful for the help Oscar was willing to give, and I didn't take it lightly. Being a woman in an industry run by men was, well, just like living in a world run by men.

"Getting in the door is half the battle, Oscar. I can handle the rest! Thank you!" I gave him a huge hug and kissed him on the cheek. I looked over to Rose to get her reaction. She gave me a big smile and nodded her head in approval, and affectionately wrapped her arms around Oscar.

Ted, who was full of jokes that night, seemed to get quiet. I wondered what that was about. I hoped he didn't think I was crazy for trying to go after my dream again, after all that had happened. I pushed that thought out of my head as I looked up to the shining lights of the marquees in Times Square.

CHAPTER 14

FILL MY CUP

——

AUDREY: AUDREY'S HOUSE, SUMMER—1990

I don't know why we as women tend to lean into that traditional notion of being caretakers. I mean, for my generation, that was the expectation of us, and we didn't really have other choices. I went to college and eventually went back to work as a music teacher, but that was long after spending twenty-plus years raising my children.

For the first time in over forty years, I realized just how tired I was from playing the caretaker role. Was it possible to have post-traumatic sleep deprivation kick in? Because I was exhausted. There was a saying about putting your oxygen mask on first, the one they'd tell people on airplanes. Well, after my husband died, I had finally put on my oxygen mask and started taking care of myself first.

Fill My Cup

AUDREY
I haven't had sleep like this
I can't remember when

Rolling out of bed at ten
Not a sound in the house
no one to cook
clean or care for
and therefore
I get to just

Fill my cup
Fill my cup
No one else can feed
The passion that I need
So I'm just taking care of me

I put on my cozy red bathrobe and headed to the kitchen to put the tea kettle on. It whistled and startled me from the silence. I turned the burner off and reached for a teacup and saucer with tiny green shamrocks on it that Rose gave me for my birthday. I placed an Earl Grey tea bag into the cup, poured the steaming hot water in, took a sip, and exhaled. Oh, the simplicity of a cup of tea in silence.

While silence could be a beautiful sound, it was almost deafening, and I had a sudden urge to play the piano. No one was there, so why not play at ten o'clock in the morning? I wouldn't be waking anyone up! I had bought myself a small electric keyboard, and while it didn't have the same sound quality as my piano, at least I could still play.

Chopin and Gershwin and Bach
each chord slowly unlocks
the keys to my favorite melodies
not a soul in the house
no one to bake, bed, or buy for

and therefore
I can just

Fill my cup
Fill my cup
No one else can feed
The passion that I need
So I'm just taking care of me

Mother, Grandmother, Wife
each role defined my life
There's a woman inside that's still me
And I really like what I see
I'm embracing each part
complex bold and beautiful
pieces of art
shape my identity

So I will keep
Filling my cup
Filling my cup
I'm taking my time
getting to know
How to just take care of me

So how could I fill my own cup exactly? What did I even want to do? I enjoyed the peace and quiet and simplicity of my life, and if I wanted to do nothing, I could, although I was not very good at sitting still. Why do nothing when I could do something I'd never done before? Rose and I had been talking about a trip to Australia.

A former student of mine, Suzie Zimmer, now a young woman, had told me about the Bernstein piano competition and that some of her students would be competing in it in Australia. Finding unique pianos, seeing the piano competition in person, and getting to see Suzie after all these years all sounded so incredible. I deserved it, right? I would get to create my own adventures.

I picked up the brochure about the piano competition from the table, and I could hear Australia calling me. *'If not now, when?'* I thought.

"I'm taking myself on a trip!" I replied to my empty kitchen. Just saying it out loud sounded so exciting.

Pianos were waiting for me!

BERNSTEIN PIANO COMPETITION, AUSTRALIA—1990

The concert hall was cavernous, like a cave with the most amazing acoustics. There was a nervous energy in the air with parents, grandparents, and piano teachers waiting patiently for the competition to begin. I had my own nervous excitement to see Suzie. She was a naturally gifted pianist as a young girl, with an extremely dedicated work ethic for her age. She won this competition as a teen and moved to Australia, having fallen in love with the country, and quite frankly, I couldn't blame her.

The students were all dressed in classic black and white and sat with their legs crossed and hands in their laps, holding tight to their music. Some of their feet didn't even reach the floor yet. One little girl, who couldn't be more than eight, had her blond hair in a beautiful French braid, and her fingers were moving in the air, imagining the keys. A nervous habit, but also one I'd done myself many times.

It was a practicing tactic. You heard the song in your head and visualized the keys. Sometimes it was truly an unconscious response when your fingers started moving in the air, following along with the music in your head. Many children who learned to play piano at an early age started purely by ear before they could even read music.

I taught piano lessons to the children at the elementary school where I taught, and some of my own grandchildren. The afternoons when I had little budding musicians sitting next to me on the piano bench were some of my favorite moments. Their little fingers exploring the keys for the first time, their legs not long enough to reach the pedals and just hanging off the bench, and the pride that beamed out of them when they played their first song. I thought fondly of my grandchildren and piano students back home.

The Bernstein Master of Ceremonies made an introduction and urged everyone to find their seats and to welcome the participants in that year's competition. The younger students performed first, which was smart. Let the little ones get it over with first. It must have been hard for them to sit still waiting in anticipation. I was routing for the blond with the French braid. An incredibly confident redheaded boy covered in freckles practically marched up the stairs and took his seat at the piano. He made a show of flipping his music over to show the audience and the judges he had memorized it by heart. Good for him, but foolish, I thought. There was nothing wrong with reading music, and what if he lost his place in his mind? I was nervous for him.

He played Mozart's "Piano Sonata Number 18 in D major", and I held my breath. That was one of the most difficult pieces to play. His staccato was strong, and his trills flowed effortlessly. Then about a third of the way through, I saw the panic set in on this face.

He was lost.

He took his fingers off the keys, reached for his music, and flipped it back forward and quickly searched for his place, and picked up where he left off. Noticeably rattled, and his fingers were shaking, but he got the ground back under him and finished the piece strong. He picked up his music and walked down the stairs without the confident march he started with—poor thing. Hubris could really mess with all good intentions.

The blond with the French braid was next, and I found myself sitting up straighter in my seat and leaning forward. I didn't even know this girl, but somehow, I felt a connection to her. I checked the program and skimmed that she picked a Debussy piece, "Estampes, Pagodes." I loved Debussy.

She took her seat and inhaled with the most precious smile. She appeared excited with the right mix of nerves. I closed my eyes and said a little prayer for her.

With my eyes still closed, the notes were creating the most beautiful painting in my mind. It was a watercolor, and each note was like a paintbrush adding new pastels to the canvas with each stroke. Then the painting shifted, and the notes were like rain falling. The rain washed over the audience with a hush. Now the pitter-patter of the rain transformed again into airy lightness, and I pictured ballet dancers gliding across the stage, their bodies moving gracefully through the air. The tempo picked up, and I could see butterflies flying in a field of bright yellow sunflowers, their wings flapping and swirling. The crescendo grew with such power and elegance and then softened like pink rose petals gently floating and falling from the sky.

Then suddenly, the rose petals faded into the distance, and there was silence. I could feel the tears streaming down my face, and I wasn't sure when they had started. A mix of pure joy and pain all tangled up together in one breathtaking piece of music. Music heals. I stood and clapped, as did the other audience members. I didn't care what the other pieces sounded like. This girl had won in my mind.

A tissue was suddenly being handed to me, and startled, I looked to my left. There was Suzie with a big grin on her face, holding the tissue out to me. I laughed and gave her a huge hug.

"She was spectacular, wasn't she?" Suzie asked.

"Beyond. For once in my life, I'm speechless."

"Layla. She's one of my best students. Such a hard worker. Never stops practicing, and boy does she have spunk."

"She sounds a lot like her teacher," I said, smirking.

"Takes one to know one," Suzie smirked right back.

"Ha. It's so good to see you. You haven't changed a bit."

"Thanks, Mrs. M."

"Please, call me Audrey! You are a grown woman now."

"I'll try, but you'll always be Mrs. M. to me."

"Suit yourself. Do you think you might have time to do some piano hunting with me this week?"

"Piano hunting?"

"I was reading about Wertheim pianos. They originated in Melbourne, and they built about eighteen thousand between 1908 and 1935. I thought it would be neat to find one while I'm here."

"Wow. Okay, well, you know I love a challenge. Let me make some calls to some of the boutique piano dealers in town. That should be a good start."

"Thank you, Suzie!" I squealed with delight. "Let the piano treasure hunting begin!"

"You got it. I'll come to find you after the competition."

I took my seat and listened to the rest of the competition. One by one, they each were more talented than the next. None of them moved me the way Layla did, though. There was a brief ten-minute intermission while the judges deliberated.

I could hardly believe my ears when they didn't say Layla's name as the winner and the little redheaded boy with the freckles, who got lost midpiece, took first prize!

There must have been a terrible mistake, and Layla looked crushed. Suzie was taking deep breaths trying not to curse at the judges of such a prestigious event. The redhead did choose a harder piece of music, but Layla had painted us a watercolor with her notes. I was heartbroken for her and reminded yet again it wasn't always talent that won. I glanced down at the program and saw the connection. The redhead had the same last name as the sponsor of the competition and one of the judges.

Layla probably didn't even have a shot at winning regardless of how well she played. There were so many factors outside of anyone's control. What I could control was my search for the Wertheim piano, and maybe the hunt would be even more fun than finding the treasure itself.

If only I'd had that same mindset as a young woman auditioning in New York.

CHAPTER 15

BLEND IN

———

AUDREY: NEW YORK AUDITION, FALL—1942

Words are powerful. They imprint in your brain and heart, and no matter how hard you try to erase them, they seem to get etched in even darker ink.

I went on so many auditions I lost count a long time ago. Just when you think you've figured out how to let the rejection bounce off of you, you hear something that causes you to doubt who you are, what you do, and why you wanted to do it in the first place.

I was twenty-one years old and full of determination. Leaving my cousin Rose's apartment on the Upper West Side, I took in the view of Central Park. It screamed autumn in New York as the leaves were just starting to turn, with yellows blending into golds and reds blending into burnt oranges. I wasn't sure where one color started, and another ended.

The beauty of nature was such a stark contrast to the industrial brick and gray stone buildings surrounding it. Rows of black cars were parked along the street, matching the black hats of men briskly walking to their destinations. The crisp fall air was clouded with the second-hand smoke from several New Yorkers, both businessmen and young women, as they walked past me. I waved the smoke away, carefully trying not to inhale. I didn't want that smoke in my lungs right before I had to sing.

The cheery yellow taxi cabs zipped by as my toes crunched on fresh fallen leaves. I kept humming my audition song to myself as my fingers played imaginary piano keys in the air. I had picked "Lemonade" as my audition song because we all could have used a dose of positivity those days. Its lyrics and upbeat tempo reminded you no matter what life threw your way. You could always choose to make the best of it.

I might have been humming a bit louder than I thought when an old lady carrying multiple grocery bags bumped into me.

"What are you so happy about? Did you forget we're at war?" she barked.

"Of course not! I'm just excited to audition today."

She'd already pushed past me, but I was not gonna let some grouchy old lady ruin my day. I made my way up Eighth Avenue and looked up at the big gray building I'd been to so many times before, hoping and praying this time the outcome might be different. I took the elevator up to the fifth floor, walked into the waiting room, signed in, and tried not to look at the competition. Though how could I not? Everyone looked the same. Lines of women with perfectly coiffed curls, long, lean dancer legs with black character shoes, and a sea of hour-glass silhouette dresses in cheerfully bright, primary colors.

I took out my compact and reapplied my signature shade of All-Day Rich and Rosy Lipstick to match my cranberry red dress while I waited. When they called my name, I stood with grace and confidence and walked into the audition room, holding my music.

"Hi, I'm Audrey," I said with a smile as I walked toward the piano and sat down.

Two older gentlemen in gray suits matching their salt and pepper hair sat behind a table strewn with paper coffee cups and an ashtray filled with cigarette butts. So much for avoiding smoke. Their heads were buried in paperwork, though one of them acknowledged me with a slight head nod. I took that as my cue to keep going, opened my music, placed my fingers on the keys, and belted out the first few bars.

"And when life gives me lemons, I'm making lemonade!" For those few moments, I was completely in tune with myself. I felt alive and grateful to be playing the piano and singing my heart out. Being at a piano always made me feel at home. Placing my fingers on the keys was like planting my feet on the ground.

The casting director let me finish the last note of the phrase and, leaning in with what seemed like earnest interest, said, "Thanks, doll. Do you dance?"

Without thinking, I responded honestly. "Well, no sir, I play the piano, and I sing."

He turned his head, let out a condescending "hmph," and replied, "I need singers who can dance and *blend,* not piano players who can sing."

There it was. Words that were imprinted on my brain and starting to chip away at my confidence.

"Girls who can play the piano don't fill seats. Girls who can dance and sing fill seats. Frankly, if you can't do that, you're not gonna make it in this business," he continued.

I felt the blow like a punch in the gut, but my anger fueled my courage.

"Well, think what you want. I know I've got more moxie than those girls! You have a killer-diller day!"

I slapped on a confident smile through gritted teeth, grabbed my music, and booked it out of the audition room before they could respond. Beneath my sassy remarks and fake smile, my crushed inner child quietly asked, '*Why do they always want me to blend in?*'

It was a question I would later ask myself and Rose when I found myself back in her apartment, collapsed on the black velvet couch as she poured me a cup of tea; our way to commiserate another failed attempt at chasing my dream. My eyes wandered to the carved black swans that flanked the corners of the couch. Their necks are long and graceful, but their painted red beaks are looking down at the ground. I couldn't help but feel like those swans as my finger traced over their necks, graceful, different, powerful, but unsure of themselves. They didn't blend in either.

"Can you believe he said that to me?"

"Unfortunately, I can believe it. There is a lot wrong with this industry. But don't listen to those knuckleheads. They'll be sorry they missed out on booking you!" Rose said, trying to cheer me up.

"Why do they want me to blend in?"

"I don't know, Audrey. But if they can't appreciate you for who you are, then they don't deserve your talent."

"I guess I'll just have to keep trying until someone does," I sighed.

"Yes! It takes a lot of courage to keep trying. Giving up would be so much easier, but you don't. You just keep persisting, and I'm so proud of you for that. "

"Thank you. It's just so frustrating to feel like you have no control over the outcome."

"Yes, but isn't that so much of our lives? Feeling like we have no control over the outcome?"

"Yes! I wish I could just click my heels or wave a magic wand."

"Oh, me too, but magic wands aren't real. *You* are real, Audrey, and your talent is *real*. So, what *do* you have control over?" Rose asked.

"Well, I guess I can keep practicing, so I'm ready for the next time."

"Yes, that's the spirit! Now, why don't you play me the whole song you didn't get to finish. I'd love to hear it." I sat up and grinned at Rose, happy to have her unwavering support. I could always count on her to help lift my mood after a failed audition.

"Special performance just for you, coming up! As I played the song for Rose, the keys grounded me again. My fingers felt light as a feather as I played and remembered myself as the little girl at the piano, determined to learn.

And learn I did, with my brother Bobby at my side. I would keep chasing my dream, not just for me, but for my brother and the dreams he never got to chase. I wasn't going to give up. I would keep auditioning.

ANOTHER AUDITION, FALL—1942

"I can do this. I can do this," I said to myself. My hair was perfect, lipstick on, and dress pressed with a girdle underneath, cinching my waist. The heels I'd picked were not comfortable, but they made my legs look good. I'd chosen beauty over comfort. I had even gotten up extra early that day to practice and warm up, and I'd had two cups of steaming hot tea with honey and lemon, so my voice was awake and ready.

I was planning to try something different for this particular audition. I had decided not to play to piano and was just going to sing. Maybe that would make me seem like I "blended more" and wasn't trying to be all the things, just one thing. Just a singer.

It seemed like I was hiding a piece of myself by doing that, but wasn't that what show business was all about? Hiding behind other people's words, and phrases, and music? I would act and think like I was just a singer, so therefore, I was.

When they called my name, I entered the audition space and walked confidently to the center of the room. I introduced myself to the casting director and then sang my song with all the charm and pizzazz I could, being sure to make eye contact with the casting director for the one millisecond he was looking at me.

Lemonade

Life is sweet
it's no secret
Everyone you meet
Has a moment they'd rather
not repeat

I put the turkey
in the oven
made the gravy too
apple, pumpkin, pecan pies
just to name a few
I forgot to turn the oven on
It's funny, but it's true
We had apple pie for dinner, wouldn't you?

Cuz when life gives me lemons
I'm making lemonade
Yes, when life gives me lemons
I'm making lemon—

I was about to sing the money note, took a big breath from my diaphragm, and stopped when the casting director interrupted me before I could even finish.

"Thank you, that's enough."

"Okay, thank you, but I wasn't finished..."

"Yeah, doll, you were." He went back to looking at his papers as if I wasn't even there.

As if I didn't just sing my heart out.

But that didn't really matter. I was just another brunette who could sing. I was a dime a dozen in this city. Deflated, I walked out, but I'd be damned if I let the other women waiting in the holding room see my defeat. I lifted my chin up and smiled like I had just got the part, took out my compact, powdered my nose, and reapplied my lipstick.

Once I was safely out of the building away from my competition, my stomach growled loudly. All that singing of pie and not eating enough before my audition, I suddenly knew where I wanted to go to forget this day.

CHAPTER 16

WHIPPED CREAM AND A SIDE OF PIE

AUDREY: A NEW YORK DINER, FALL—1942

Another day, another failed audition. I honestly didn't know why I kept going back for more torture. Did I honestly expect a different outcome? Wasn't that the definition of insanity? Doing the same thing over and over and expecting a different outcome?

Well, you couldn't stop a girl from dreaming! I knew I shouldn't be splurging on pie. Lord knows my waist was not going to get smaller from that, but it had been one heck of a day, and all I wanted was a big slice of apple pie. The waitress brought me a bowl of whipped cream, and I piled it on higher and higher and then took a huge bite.

"More whipped cream Miss?" the waitress asked, eyeing my leaning tower of pie and whipped cream.

"If it isn't too much trouble, and maybe a scoop of vanilla ice cream?"

"Coming right up." She walked back to the black and white checkered counter lined with turquoise stools to put in my order.

I shoved another bite into my mouth when suddenly, in walked Ted. What was he doing there?

"Audrey!" he said, and his cheeks flushed a bit. I wondered if mine flushed too. "What a nice surprise." He had caught me midmouthful with a whipped cream mustache, and I covered my mouth with my napkin, mortified to be caught red-handed. I normally picked at food like a bird, but that day I was shoveling it in like I might never get to eat again!

"Mmhmm," was my less than eloquent reply. I mumbled while I tried to chew as fast as I could. Of all the diners in New York, he had walked into the one where I was clearly trying to drown my sorrows in whipped cream!

"That looks good. Mind if I join you?" he asked, fumbling with his wallet and keys.

I did mind, but that would have been rude of me to say, and I was sure I wasn't going to be very good company sitting there feeling sorry for myself. I just needed some time alone to think. I wanted to go through the audition again in my head and see what I could've done differently, and I was sure Ted wouldn't understand or want to hear about all of that. I also hoped he didn't want to talk about what had happened between us either because that would've just been awkward. I wouldn't even know what to say. It was best to tell him it just wasn't a good day for me.

Instead, I smiled and lied through my teeth.

"Umm, sure, yes, please sit."

"So, how have you been, Audrey? I feel like we haven't talked like really talked in a long time," Ted said as he sat down in the turquoise and white striped vinyl booth opposite from me.

"Busy. I've been really, really, busy. You know, I—"

"Yeah, I'm sure you've been dealing with a lot. I, uh… you know, we should probably talk about—"

"I started auditioning again!" I blurted out before he could finish.

"Oh, that's great, about the auditions."

"Not so great, actually," I said as I looked down at the pie and immediately regretted getting it. "Here, have the rest. I clearly have had too much already." I pushed my plate of pie over to him, and our hands touched for a second.

He started to twitch as our hands touched, and then suddenly, he sneezed, causing his glasses to fall straight into the whipped cream below. I covered my mouth immediately, trying and failing to contain my laughter. It wasn't polite to laugh at your friend, but the moment was funny. I mean, really funny.

"Well, I guess it's a classic glasses in whipped cream kind of day." He shook his head and then picked up his glasses covered in whipped cream and put them back on his face without so much as cracking a smile. I could not stop the laughter from coming, and soon enough, tears started to run down my face.

Why had I thought that him sitting down was going to make my day worse again?

"Thank you, Ted."

"For what?"

"For cheering me up. You always seem to be there when I need a friend." I leaned over the table and carefully took his glasses off, and we both just looked at each other for a moment. The man looking back at me was strong, steady, kind, funny, and *there*, right in front of me. He touched my bottom lip to wipe some of the whipped cream off and then leaned in and gently kissed me. This time, I didn't push him away.

"Of course. Happy to be of service." I smiled back at him and realized I was happy. I had almost forgotten why I needed the pie in the first place.

I was just too scared to admit what I was trying to ignore. I liked Ted, and the truth was, I really hoped he'd kiss me again.

AUDREY: JANE'S HOUSE, THANKSGIVING—1992

I was so dependent on men back then. I wrapped up my whole identity in the men in my life, who they were, who I was when I was with them, and how they loved me. Their love had defined me. Did I even have a clue about who I was without being loved by Vic, or Ted, or Dr. O?

Then there was Bobby, and his love was the most important to me of all.

Searching for pianos has given me time to search for myself, and I have realized if I can't love myself, why should anyone else? Remembering those big moments—the heartbreaking ones—I can see my life as a tapestry woven together with pinks and purples, deep reds, and cobalt blues. Each stitch creates a new pattern, and one thread is as important as the next.

In some places, the colors might not look like they go together on the surface, as if they might seem too bold or too bright to blend in a gorgeous tapestry. Just like two notes played together that sound dissonant at first, but then your ear adjusts to the sound, and you realize it's beautiful.

I realize life is like that. The big, bold, bright colors can live in harmony with the gray, and it's beautiful to me. I take in my granddaughter Amelia's face and how she has been hanging on my every word as I tell her my story. She might also experience some of these things in her own life, and I can only hope she finds it just as beautiful.

CHAPTER 17

PERMISSION SLIP

"And then he dropped his glasses in the whipped cream!" Audrey said.

I was only half-listening. My thoughts were wandering, but I wanted so badly to hear about her and Ted. Ever since he had shown up drunk to the apartment, I had been worried about both of them. Still, I couldn't help but think about everything that had been happening in my own life.

"He didn't!" I exclaimed.

"He did!"

I was proud of Ted. He was doing exactly what we talked about. He was being her friend and being there for her. She hadn't smiled and laughed like that in months. With Vic leaving and losing Bobby, I just didn't know how much more heartbreak she could take. It had been a hard few months for her. She needed some light in her life right now. I had hoped having her over would lift her spirits a bit.

"You have been spending a lot of time with Ted," I mentioned as I walked over to the black lacquer china cabinet to get us two teacups. I kept my good china with the gold lace trim there. I'd always liked a more clean and modern aesthetic and decorated the apartment in all black and white furniture with accents of gold. Oscar's piano was the centerpiece of the living room, with framed pictures of the latest Broadway stars he'd discovered resting on top. Everything was in its place, neat and tidy.

I gently picked up the white teacups and matching saucers out of the cabinet. I knew it was just a Thursday afternoon, but why not use the fancy china for Audrey. She deserved it. I grabbed the box of scones, cookies, and pastries I'd picked up from the bakery earlier and made sure to have the Linzer tart cookies with the raspberry filling. I knew those were her favorite.

"We're friends. He's been incredibly kind to me." I wondered just how kind he had been as I took a bite of chocolate scone. How had I ended up in the middle of this anyway? Somehow, I was rooting for Ted. I put a cookie on a plate for Audrey and handed it to her. She smiled at the sight of her favorite cookie.

"I know." I didn't want to push or be too obvious with my nudging. I wanted her to be happy, to follow her dream of the stage without worrying about how she was going to provide for herself.

I'd seen so many young actors and actresses in our circle in between gigs, and it was not a pretty picture. The unmarried women had to make hard choices to survive. Choices I never wanted to see Audrey have to make. Since Vic hadn't proposed or married her before leaving, she had no safety net.

War brides were provided for and received government assistance if their husbands died in the line of duty. If something happened to Vic, Audrey would get nothing except more heartbreak and hard times. Ted could provide for her, and he loved her. She needed to come to her own realization about Ted in her own time, but if I could help her see the possibility, I didn't think that could hurt.

"You look tired," I said, trying to be kind. She looked awful like she hadn't slept in weeks.

"I didn't sleep last night."

"Why not? I thought you and Ted got home early." I couldn't resist! I could tell she had a lot on her mind, and she wasn't telling me everything. I'd get it out of her eventually. I always did.

"I was up thinking about Ted—Vic! I mean Vic." Bingo. He was on her mind! Nice work, Ted. I gave her a knowing glance.

"Vic, right, did you get a letter?"

"No. It's been seven months."

I sat down on the couch next to her and put my arm around her to comfort her. Seven months was a long time not to hear from the love of your life. I knew we were at war, and nothing was guaranteed, let alone reliable mail, but I still didn't understand why he hadn't at least proposed before he left. Somehow that type of promise would've made the waiting more bearable for her, I think.

She leaned her head on my shoulder for a minute and said softly, as if admitting it for the first time, "I don't think he's coming home."

"You don't?"

"I don't think he's coming home," she said decisively. We sat there in silence. Her eyes darted side to side, and she looked off to the right like she would when she was deep in thought. I knew she was processing this sudden realization, and I needed to give her time and space to do that in her way.

"I don't want to keep waiting. I don't think I can keep waiting."

"Waiting for Vic?" I asked.

"No. Waiting for life!" she exclaimed and threw her hands up in the air.

"Audrey, you are living life! You've been auditioning without Vic!" I reminded her and matched her intensity.

"Yes and failing miserably. I'm not a chorus girl," she said. "I'm a serious musician, and they don't take women seriously. That casting director didn't even let me finish my song. He just cut me off mid-note. Can you believe that?"

"I take you seriously, and you are not failing Audrey. You are pursuing your dream. It was never supposed to be easy."

"Everything seemed easy with Vic here. Now I'm going to be an old maid. No love. No music. No children. I'm not like you, Rose. I want a family. You and Oscar have such a full life without kids, but I want them."

"Well, you seem to know exactly what you want and are making a lot of assumptions. There is no reason why you can't have all of those things." Did she think we wanted it that way?

Of course, I wanted children, but I was too scared to try again. As close as we were, there were some things that Audrey didn't need to know, and yet I was surprised she hadn't asked or put two and two together on her own. Talking about this made me uneasy, and I needed to change the subject. We were here to talk about her life choices, not mine.

"What do you mean?" Audrey asked.

"It seems to me you have life staring you in the face. Did you or did you not go out with an attractive, young soldier last night?" There was no holding back now.

"Ted is Vic's best friend."

"So?"

"What kind of a woman would I be if I dated his best friend while he's away at war? I'd be breaking a promise to Vic."

I could tell that Audrey needed permission from someone to move on. I was happy to give it to her.

"I don't know. I can't give you a good answer. Ugh... This is so hard, but you might need to just keep your eyes and heart open. There's so much going on right now in the world. I know *I* wouldn't judge you for not waiting. And besides, you said it yourself. You don't know if Vic is ever coming home. But Ted is home, and he's a good man. Just think about that."

"I'm not denying he's a good man. But he's not Vic."

"Of course, and he'll never replace Vic. I know you don't want to think about this, Audrey, but we are at war. There might not be a lot of eligible husbands in the future, depending on how long our men are overseas. A lot of women your age snatched up the good ones before they left, and they will provide for them."

"What are you saying?"

"I'm saying you need to think about your future. If you want to go after Carnegie, like I know you do, you need someone to provide for you, and I've seen the way Ted looks at you. I think maybe you're starting to look at him too."

"I can never seem to hide anything from you," Audrey replied, sounding almost amused. "I love Vic. I love Vic more than anything, and yet, Ted seems to be creeping into my heart, and I can't stop it." Her shoulders, heavy with guilt, released as she confessed both of these truths.

"So don't stop it," I replied.

"Maybe I won't."

CHAPTER 18

HOLY CANNOLI

———

AUDREY: SAINT MICHAEL'S HOSPITAL, FALL—1991

I peered through the glass of the nursery when I heard someone behind me ask, "Which one is yours?"

"Oh, not mine, my grandson, Oliver." I turned, beyond flattered that someone thought I was young enough to have a new baby.

"Congratulations! My God, Audrey, you haven't aged a bit!" Dr. O said, surprised.

"Dr. O'Connor! What a welcome surprise!" I said. I couldn't believe the coincidence running into him at the hospital. It was jarring to see him in any other context than delivering one of my kids. I don't think I ever saw Dr. O outside of the hospital or his office when I was either newly pregnant, very pregnant, delivering a baby, or some moments in between. His eyes and brow had aged a bit, and yet his wrinkles made him look even more distinguished and wise. I had never really noticed before how handsome he was either, but he was.

"Likewise. How's your husband?" he asked.

"I'm afraid he's no longer with us. He passed two years ago."

"I'm so sorry to hear that. My wife Catherine lost her fight with cancer last year."

"I'm sorry for your loss."

So we both had lost our spouses. I wondered how he had managed without Catherine taking care of him. Not that anyone was taking care of me, but it was different for men, and he was a doctor. He had a big important job. I'm sure Catherine had handled everything at home so he could focus on his work. That's what doctor's wives did, or all wives from our generation anyway.

"Thank you. It is incredibly quiet at home. How do you spend your time with the kids all grown?"

"Oh, I sing in the choir, teach piano lessons, spend time with my grandchildren… but dinner time always seems the hardest."

"Well, I hope you don't find this too forward, but would you like to have dinner this Saturday? The San Gennaro festival is this weekend." This was both unexpected and exciting. I was just starting to get used to life without a man, but it would be nice to go out with someone I had so much history with.

We both had to eat anyway, so it was just a harmless dinner between old friends if you could call us that. I guess I was more of a patient than a friend. I did love Italian food, and I hated cooking dinner for one. What could it hurt?

"Well, that sounds just lovely," I answered.

"It's a date then! I'll pick you up at seven."

"Paging Dr. O'Connor, Paging Dr. O'Connor"

Dr. O gestured to the loudspeaker. "That's me."

"A date on Saturday it is," I said as he started to walk down the hall. He turned to wave before disappearing around a corner.

Holy cannoli. I was going on a date, a real date, with a real man and a doctor at that! *My* doctor, in fact. I couldn't even remember how to act on a date. It had been so long, and I wasn't a young woman anymore. Were the rules still the same? Should I play hard to get? Did I need to bat my eyes and compliment him like crazy? Who was I kidding? He'd probably think there was something in my eye if I did that.

I was ridiculous. I just needed to be myself.

LITTLE ITALY, DATE NIGHT—1991

It was a warm September night, the kind of night that felt like it was still summer, but I had put a light sweater around my shoulders just in case it got chilly later. He arrived with yellow tulips, which were so thoughtful. I quickly put them in a vase with some water, and then Dr. O drove us into the city. He put the radio on and rolled the windows down while we drove, and I was thankful for the sound. I wasn't ready to dive into conversation yet.

After we had parked the car and started walking toward the festival, Dr. O said, "I thought we could skip the formal sit-down dinner so we can try lots of food options at the festival. Is that all right?"

"Sounds great! Why tie ourselves down to one," I said and thought walking would help with my nerves as opposed to just sitting across from each other for an hour.

"Great minds think alike. Let's get us a drink. I heard they make a killer sangria." We stopped at a sangria stand,

and each got a glass. The sangria had the most delicious little chunks of peaches, apples, and oranges that were just the right combination of sweet mixed with the rich red wine.

We walked through the San Genaro Festival, drinking our sangria as we stopped and explored the different food vendors. I could've eaten my way through the festival, but it was our first date! I needed to restrain myself, so I picked delicately, but oh my God, the smells were intoxicating. The mix of fried cheese deliciousness, sausage and peppers on the grill, and fried dough and powdered sugar were wafting through my nose, and I could feel my stomach growling in response.

In the center of the festival was a small stage with a piano and a three-piece band that alternated between playing traditional classical Italian music to Frank Sinatra standards from my day. Oh, how we all loved Frankie back then. The singer was crooning away to "Come Fly with Me," and I was humming along and tapping my foot. I didn't know what to talk about with Dr. O, and I enjoyed taking in the music, but I could sense it was time for the real date to begin. He cleared his throat nervously several times and kept shifting his weight from side to side.

"So, did you always want to be a doctor?" I asked.

"Actually, no. I dreamed of being a firefighter."

"Well, I could've put you to work in my kitchen!"

"Your kitchen?" Dr. O asked. He then handed me a warm zeppole out of a brown paper bag.

"Let's just say there were many dinners that ended with the smoke alarm going off."

I took a tiny bite of the zeppole, and it was pure heaven. "Mmm... wow, you have got to try this."

Dr. O reached into the bag, pulled out a zeppole, and took a bite. Powdered sugar dust flew out like a cloud of smoke, and we both laughed. The ice seemed broken. His hands were shaking a bit, though, and I realized he was nervous, too, which was both endearing and a relief.

"Mmm... I can't imagine cooking for thirteen kids. There had to be constant interruptions!"

"Interruptions, food fights, crying babies, hungry toddlers, moody teenagers, just to name a few. But enough about the chaos of my kitchen, why a firefighter?"

"I was always fascinated with the idea of saving people."

"Well, you certainly saved me many times, through many fires."

"That's very sweet of you to say, Audrey, but I was just doing my job."

"Now, don't be modest, You did save my life, and I don't think I ever said thank you."

"You are very welcome." The band started playing "Fly Me to the Moon," and I found myself swaying side to side. I took a sip of liquid courage from my cup.

"Would you like to dance?" I bravely asked him.

"Of course! Let me just get rid of this wine." Dr. O put our sangrias and zeppole's down on a nearby table set up for the festival, and I grabbed his hand and pulled him onto the dance floor.

I transported back to the forties and suddenly felt young again. We swung along to the beat and did a little two-step. He was a good dancer! He twirled me and dipped me, and I was smiling ear to ear. Then the swing turned slower, and he pulled me closer, and I instinctively put my head on his shoulder. It had been a long time since I was this close to a man. He smelled like clean ivory soap mixed with rain. I had goosebumps, and the closeness of the moment was interrupted when he looked down and broke the silence.

"I know it seems like an obvious question, but did you always want to be a mother?"

"Yes, I did. I just didn't want to be the kind of mom my mother was. I wanted more than that."

"What did you want more of?"

"More of life. More music, more love, more adventure."

"And what's stopping you now from getting those things?"

"That's a great question," I said. There was a lull in the music, and the crowd turned their heads to the stage.

"Do we have any performers in the crowd tonight?" The band leader said into the microphone.

"Audrey, that's you."

"You're funny, Dr. O. I haven't played in front of people in years," I said.

"We're getting ready to do a crowd favorite, 'New York, New York,' come on up if you want to sing with us." The bandleader asked one more time. As he started to play the first few chords, I felt the courage coming into my fingers as the familiar notes and melody rang in my ear. The anthem of the city of dreams. My city. My dreams.

"You look like you want to go up there," he said.

"I do but, I'm afraid…" I said nervously, avoiding his eyes.

"More music, more adventure. Go for it." He smiled at me, and I found myself returning it.

I gathered up my nerve and boldly walked right up to the stage and whispered to the piano player, "I got this." I played and sang my heart out, and the crowd cheered and clapped. I hadn't performed like that for an audience in a very, very long time. The applause was a delightful surprise and a reminder I was still a performer and always would be, no matter how old I was.

After the song was over, I made my way down the stairs of the stage and couldn't stop smiling. Dr. O looked at me in awe. "Wow. You were fantastic," he remarked.

"Thank you!" I replied, breathless with joy.

"How did that feel?"

"Invigorating!"

"I gotta say, Audrey, I didn't know what to expect tonight. It's been a long time, and yet..."

You're So Much More

Dr. O
Delightful conversation
With an interesting twist
reveal a secret musician
Playing in our midst
Your energy is contagious
Yet completely unaware
As your melodies engage us
How can I possibly compare?

Wife and mother
roles you've patiently played
Husband and doctor
professions prudently displayed
but seeing your actions aligned with your joy
expose the concessions I've made; oh boy

I thought I knew who you were
Thought I knew what you wanted

Thought I knew who I was
I thought I knew what I started
You're not what I was looking for
You're so much more

You need Paris in the springtime
London in the fall
Hawaii in the summer
We'll experience it all
Risks are out there for the taking
if you're willing
We'll be an adventure in the making

You're not what I was looking for
You're so much more

"Oh, my goodness, don't make me blush, Dr. O'Connor." I smiled at him. I couldn't believe all the wonderful things he just sang to me, but this was only our first date. I knew I felt something when we were dancing, but this seemed too fast.

There was a long awkward pause, and I could see his wheels turning when he blurted out, "Have you ever been to Paris?

"Paris? No, I haven't. I actually just got back from Australia."

"Australia, wow, you'll have to tell me all about it, in Paris."

"Are you asking me to go to Paris with you?" This was all moving extremely fast. It was our first date, but how incredibly romantic. Who could say no to Paris? I bet there were some incredibly rare pianos to be found there. I'd already been to Australia, Europe could be next, and then... oh, I was getting ahead of myself.

"Yes! Let's go on an adventure!"

"Well, you are full of surprises, Dr. O'Connor."

"A good surprise or a bad surprise?"

"Paris is always a good surprise, but…" What would people think of him and me traveling together? A widow and a widower traveling to the most romantic city in the world. We would have to have separate rooms, of course. I didn't want him getting the wrong idea.

"Shoot. I went too fast. I'm sorry. I got swept up in the moment."

"No, no, my logical brain is just kicking in." I paused for a moment before turning a bright grin on him. "I just said I wanted more adventure in my life. Let's do it!"

"Really?" he sounded so excited.

"Yes. Let's go to Paris!" I reaffirmed.

"Well, I'll cheers to that!" he said happily.

My men were full of surprises, and while it took a lot to surprise me at this age, Dr. O still had a few more up his sleeve.

CHAPTER 19

THE WORLD OUTSIDE

AUDREY: CRUISE TO HAWAII, SUMMER—1992

Searching for pianos became my new hobby, and people would always ask me why pianos, like it was the strangest thing they'd ever heard. I would look at them and ask, "Why did you get a puppy after all the kids left the house?" or "Why do you collect antique teacups?" I needed something to fill the void and the quiet that an empty house brought me. The quiet made you question things.

Being alone with your thoughts could sometimes sound louder than the noise of a house exploding with thirteen kids.

I had spent my entire life raising children and taking care of everyone else. I was embarrassed to say I had never left the tristate area before. Who knew there was a whole world outside of New Jersey? Traveling to places I had never been before, researching each place and the rare pianos I might find there had been the biggest treasure hunt of my life!

I never expected I'd make new friends, let alone a friend who was a man! I always knew friendship was important to me, but not to such a great extent as I do now. All the people in my life were incredibly important to me. Rose, my kids and grandkids, Dr. O... though, of course, Dr. O was more than just a friend. Friendship was the foundation of any successful relationship, and Dr. O was a wonderful friend. He was more than a friend. Obviously, we wouldn't have gone on all these trips together if he wasn't.

We did always have separate rooms when we traveled together, and I had made it a point to tell the kids that before we left. They looked at me like, "Mom, we don't care. You're a grown woman." But I couldn't have my children or grandchildren thinking—oh God knows what they thought! Grandma was on a cruise with her boyfriend.

Even just saying it out loud sounded so silly. Maybe Dr. O was worried about the same thing. What his children and grandchildren must have thought of him traveling the world with his *girlfriend*? I knew the kids would say, "Grandma, relax, it's the 1990s!"

I was trying to relax. I really was, but relaxing was a new thing for me. I could feel the heat of the tropical sun on my face, and the hum of the cruise ship engine was surprisingly calming. The wind was whispering in my ear: "It's time for an adventure!"

As I leaned off the side of the cruise ship and sang out to the ocean, I felt the magnitude of its depth. The power of the sea, the uncertainty of the waves, of what lay beneath the surface, and all that was out there unseen to explore. My hair kept whipping about with the wind, and my eyes squinted in the bright sun as I contemplated and reveled in a moment to myself. My cherry red summer dress flounced against the side of the ship, echoing my refrain.

The World Outside

AUDREY

If I was born
In a different time
and a different place
Who would I be?
What would the culture
And the history
and the people
teach me to be?

There's a world outside
that I've never seen
There's a world outside
and places in between
there's adventure in the air
as the wind blows through my hair
There's a world outside
I just can't wait to see

I've lived my life
and raised my kids
have loved and lost
there's still more to do
I've got a new love
and a suitcase
and ticket
ready to pursue

There's a world outside
that I've never seen

There's a world outside
and places in between
there's adventure in the air
as the wind blows through my hair
There's a world outside
We finally get to see

Stain glass windows
Baguettes with wine and cheese
History of Heroes
and warm Hawaiian breeze
Mona Lisa smirks
as the lovers pass her by
Hushed cathedral hymns
Sing to towers in the sky

I wasn't born
in a different time
or a different place
but the culture
and the history
and the people
taught me to face

The world outside
that I've finally seen
the world outside
and places in between
there's adventure in the air
as the wind blows through my hair
exploring the world outside
I've discovered a new me

Caught up in my own thoughts and song, I was interrupted by a tap on my shoulder.

"More wine, Audrey?" Dr. O'Connor asked. My new partner in adventure looked like a silver-haired fox, his steely blue eyes shining with kindness as he handed me a chilled glass of chardonnay.

"I'd love some, thank you." I took a sip, and the oaky freshness instantly brought me back to the dock we had just left behind. "You know, I can't stop thinking about that antique piano we saw in Paris."

"Oh, what about it?"

"I've never seen a piano with such elaborate gold gilt accents before. Imagine the family who first bought it back in 1905! It must have cost a small fortune. "

"I'm sure you're right, Audrey. A piano alone would have been an investment, but one adorned with gold? Now that was incredibly unique."

"Indeed. Did I tell you I found one in Australia?"

"Australia? Wow. So, what exactly did you find there?"

"It was my first big trip, and I went specifically to find an original Wertheim from 1908. They're pretty rare."

"Interesting..." I could tell he was running out of things to say about the pianos, so he changed the subject to avoid getting into piano specifics. "So, what's on your mind?"

"I don't know... I mean, I really love traveling the world."

"I do too!"

"I want to keep looking for more unique pianos."

Dr. O tilted his head, puzzled. "Like a treasure hunt?" he asked.

"Yes! Exactly."

"A piano treasure hunt sounds fascinating. I—I've been doing some thinking too."

Not sure what he was about to say, I felt something in the palm of my hand. I squeezed the object, careful not to let it drop out of my fingers, lifted my fist up to look closer, and found a little black velvet box. I looked at the box and looked at him and then opened it slowly. A beautiful sparkling, antique diamond engagement ring blinded me.

"Dr. O'Connor!" I gasped.

Dr. O took my hands in his and said, "Well, I know this is unexpected, but I want to keep going on adventures with you. Would you do me the honor of becoming my wife?" he asked with eyes full of hope.

"This is wonderful. I just..." I stammered, trying to find the right words at the moment without hurting him. I was excited but also very confused. Who wouldn't be, getting proposed to at this stage in their life? I needed to think about what this decision meant before giving him an answer.

I hoped he'd respect I didn't take this decision, or marriage, lightly. "Would it... would it be all right if you gave me a little time to think about it?" I asked tentatively.

Crestfallen but diplomatic as ever, he responded, "Of course, Audrey, take all the time you need. I'll give you some time to think. I'll see you at dinner?"

"Thank you, Dr. O. Yes, see you at dinner." I wanted to kiss him goodbye, but the moment felt confusing enough as it was. He walked down the deck of the ship, and I was left alone with my thoughts to take in what had just happened.

Dr. O'Connor's wife. Wife. That title held so much weight. What was I doing? I'd been down this road before. I'd already been someone's wife, and mother, and grandmother, and I'd taken care of everyone. How did we get here so fast?

This decision felt so different from the night my husband proposed. I thought of that night often.

CHAPTER 20

WITH YOUR HAND

———

AUDREY: NEW YORK CITY NIGHTCLUB, OPENING NIGHT PARTY, WINTER—1942

I tried to listen to Rose and keep my eyes and heart open to Ted. A few months later, Ted and I were at one of Oscar's opening night parties held at a classy nightclub. Everyone was dancing, the champagne was flowing, and Rose and Oscar were gracefully dancing in almost slow motion. Ted was in his best army uniform, and oh, he looked so handsome.

I was worried about finding the perfect dress for that night, you never knew who you could meet in the entertainment world at one of Oscar's parties, but after shopping with Rose, we'd landed on a gorgeous floor-length cobalt blue with a sweetheart neckline. God, I loved that dress. I felt like a movie star that night. Rose also lent me a sapphire and pearl brooch, and I couldn't stop catching a glimpse of myself in the wall of mirrors across from the bar. I had never worn anything that expensive before in my life. I was quite pleased with the finished product.

I was sipping champagne and taking in the ambiance of the nightclub. Oscar had gone all out that night. The waiters and waitresses in their black and white uniforms bobbed and weaved throughout the crowd, filling drinks and emptying ashtrays amid the haze of smoke. The top of the bar was black onyx that must have been buffed and polished to perfection because I could practically see my reflection in it. Plush green velvet with gold stitching padded the bottom of the bar, and there were matching green velvet chairs flanked at each table with pristine white tablecloths. Was there anything classier than velvet?

A jazz quartet was playing on a stage adorned with gold curtains resembling the bustle of a woman's dress in the 1800s. The quartet played "Stardust," and Rose and Oscar were gracefully gliding across the dance floor effortlessly. The cast and crew of Oscar's latest show were all watching them in admiration. They were theater royalty.

I took another sip of my champagne and saw Ted walking toward me. His sandy blond hair was cut short, he was clean-shaven, and he seemed to have left his glasses at home. There was something incredibly attractive about a man in uniform, and Ted looked downright handsome. He was more confident in uniform, although he was more quiet than usual that night. He hadn't been making as many jokes as he usually would. Maybe he felt out of place there, but I loved being surrounded by all that glamour and rubbing elbows with a room full of creative people.

There was something different about him that night, though, something I couldn't quite put my finger on.

"Would you like to dance?" Ted asked.

"Sure."

He took my hand, led me to the dance floor, and we started to slow dance. I looked out at the crowd, and my eyes fell on a handsome-looking man with curly brown hair and freckles, and I thought of my brother fondly.

"I think Bobby would've loved this party," I said as I looked up at him.

"He would have loved watching you have a good time," Ted replied with a grin.

"And how do you know I'm having a good time?" I flirted back.

"Well, are you?" I didn't want to admit I was. The guilt had been growing in the pit of my stomach. How could I, in good conscience, be living it up in New York all dressed up and dancing with Vic's best friend while he was God knows where.

AUDREY

Worry yells in my head
another week
Praying you're not dead
and if music was a color
Without you, there is no other
The color is you
But Ted's been the armor

With Your Hand

TED

If I only had today
I would spend it with you
Just to see you smile again
And your eyes shine
The way that they do

If I only had today
I would spend it with you

Just to hear You laugh again
Oh, what I'd give to
Laugh all day with you

TED & AUDREY
We'll live like tomorrow never comes
We'll love like the
Wars already won

TED
Here I stand
I'll be the armor
Let me be the armor
With your hand

He leaned in to kiss me, and I happily lost myself in that quiet moment on the dance floor. My mind was completely at peace, and his arms felt like the armor he sang about; strong, safe, and protective.

I could've danced all night like that.

"So, what do you think? Shall we give it ago?" Ted asked.

"What are you saying?

Ted started to get down on one knee, and suddenly the room was spinning, and my heart was pounding. Every bone in my body seemed to freeze at that moment, and I held my breath.

"Audrey McKenna, you are a force to be reckoned with. I love you and will love you till the day I die. Will you marry me?"

What did I think was going to happen? I had been dating Ted for a few months, and as much as I wanted to tell myself the two of us were just friends, we were not *just* friends. Not anymore. I also couldn't just pretend Vic didn't exist because he did, and our love was real, more than real.

But this love with Ted was also real, and yet how could the two coexist?

Was it possible to love two men at the same time? It was not fair to either of them, but what choice had Vic given me? He had left. He had made his choice and had chosen not to put a ring on my finger the day he left.

Maybe he never really loved me at all.

What was I supposed to do? I had to choose. I wish I could have frozen that moment and ran to the ladies' room with Rose for some advice, but I couldn't keep Ted waiting, literally, on bended knee.

I could wait for Vic and hope he would come home, and we would pick up where we left off, following our dreams of music and settling down. But I didn't even know if he was alive. I could be waiting and waiting for nothing. I needed a husband to survive, and just like Rose had said, Ted was here, and he was a good man.

I knew he would be a wonderful husband, though our love was different. It was softer, kinder, and built on a foundation of friendship. I glanced over at Rose to try to get a read from her, and she smiled back at me, nodding ever so slightly. There was my cue.

"Yes!" I replied, "Just call me Mrs. Murphy!"

Ted jumped to his feet and lifted me up in the air, and everyone in the club started clapping. For someone who was not overly dramatic, my future husband had made quite a scene that night.

"I'll get some champagne! A toast to the happy couple!" Oscar cheered.

"You are going to make the most beautiful bride," Rose said as she kissed me and then Ted on the cheek. As she kissed Ted's cheek, I saw her whispering something in his ear. "Welcome to the family, Ted," Rose said with a huge grin, and then Oscar patted him on the back.

"Hey, I thought we already were family," Ted replied. We all laughed.

Rose clinked her champagne glass like they do at weddings, signaling the couple to kiss. Ted put his hands around my waist and pulled me to him and kissed me sweetly. Everyone clapped again, and I basked in the attention.

I was getting married! Finally! I was so excited, and yet, I hoped I was doing the right thing. A small part of me thought it should've been Vic proposing, but he was—I didn't even know where.

He would always be my first love, but who was to say you only got to have one love in life?

CHAPTER 21

MOTHER OF THE CENTURY

———

AUDREY: CARNEGIE HALL AUDITION, SPRING—1943

We were so happy, and something about marrying Ted gave me the confidence to go after Carnegie again. I know I shouldn't have needed Ted for that confidence, but I did. I finally felt loved and supported again in a way I hadn't since before Bobby had died.

We had been married for a few months when I got to audition for Carnegie. Oscar was a man of his word. He did get me in the door, several doors, in fact, throughout the previous year. Some of those doors slammed in my face, but one opened wide for me early the next year. I was a nervous wreck the night before. I must have tried on every dress I owned at least ten times, but that morning I woke up, and I shoved every bit of fear down as far as I could. I reminded myself, "I'm a girl, I'm Irish, I can do anything."

This wasn't just any audition, though. This was *the* audition. This was Carnegie Hall. I knew this time the casting directors wouldn't want me to blend in. They would want me to stand out. They were putting on a concert series featuring undiscovered women musicians, a patriotic concert to support our troops. The irony that so many of our men being away at war had created an opening for women performers was not lost on me. I was hoping this would be the opportunity I'd been waiting for. I was so excited, I barely registered my trip to Carnegie, and it wasn't till I was just about to walk on stage for my audition the feeling of excitement really sunk in.

This was the stage I'd dreamed of since I was that fiery little girl at the piano with Bobby all those years ago.

I swore I would be more than what my mother dreamed for me as I walked onto the stage. Awestruck with being in the very place I'd always wanted to be, I looked out at the empty theater, imagining wealthy patrons dressed in their most fashionable gowns and suits, whispering to each other and excited for a night of music. Rows and rows of pristine crimson velvet seats stared back at me, and the ornate gold walls sparkled under the house lights. The barren stage didn't need a set dressing since the most beautiful baby grand piano was the star set at center stage.

The casting assistant looked down at his clipboard and nodded at me. "Audrey McKenna. You're up." I had kept my maiden name for the stage to honor my brother.

I floated my way over to the piano, placed my music in front of me—though I knew it by heart, turned to the audience of one, and introduced myself.

"Hi, I'm Audrey," I said. The Casting Director glanced up from his paper and looked me straight in the eye before giving me a smile. An actual smile! While so many of my other auditions felt pointless and needed to fit in, this one felt different. I wasn't just another number.

"Good afternoon, Audrey. Please start whenever you are ready." Well, this was different. He had acknowledged my presence on the stage! I smiled to myself, hoping and praying that this time would be different, that this audition would go my way.

I turned to the piano and began to play, my voice joining in with subtle strength and power.

It's Never Too Late

AUDREY
It's never too late
To make a new dream
It's never too late
To reach for the stars
It's never too late
When the fear won't subside
It's never too late
It's never too late to try

I found myself overcome by the words of the song and the significance of what I had just achieved. I just sang and played at Carnegie Hall. Sure, it was just an audition, but I still did it. And I played and sang with all my heart. My chest tightened, and tears started to fall down my cheek. I hoped the casting director couldn't see my tears from where he was sitting, and I quickly turned my head and brushed them off my face.

The Director, who was sitting out in the middle of the house, clapped as if it was a performance and not an audition. The lights were in my eyes, so I couldn't really see him, but I could hear him.

"Thank you, that was powerful. Audrey, is it?" the Director said.

"Yes, Audrey McKenna," I replied with a slight smile. My stomach was doing flips, and I stopped breathing, unsure of what he might say next.

"When can you start?"

My heart was pounding so fast, and so loud I was worried he could hear it. I took a deep breath and squeaked out. "Uh, right away."

"Perfect. Stop by the office on your way out today, and Sam will give you the contract and rehearsal schedule."

"Okay, thank you, thank you so very much!"

With stars in my eyes, I pinched myself, started to exit the stage, and almost forgot my music at the piano. I turned back and hastily grabbed it off the piano, trying desperately to hold my excitement in. Once off stage and still holding it all in, I made my way to the ladies' room, went into a stall, and started jumping up and down like a fool. I was giddy, and I wanted to remember that moment, albeit in the bathroom stall of Carnegie Hall.

I thought all my dreams had come true. Well, that one dream had come true. Finally, someone saw me for who I was. I was not a piano player who could sing. I was not a chorus girl that should be hidden in the back blending in with all the others that looked and sounded the same. I was Audrey, a singer, a piano player, and a serious musician. I was talented and worthy of being in the spotlight. I didn't need to blend in to make my dreams come true. I'd be "All-Day Rich and Rosy" just like Bobby and I dreamed of and show my mother my uniform would be and *could* be different from hers.

CARNEGIE HALL, DRESS REHEARSAL—1943

My dream was happening!

It was the night of my big dress rehearsal at Carnegie. The shimmery red evening gown hanging in my dressing room was calling me. It was time. I carefully took it off the hanger and stepped into it and my wardrobe mistress Faye, a miracle worker with costumes, was there to help. She started to zip the dress up, but it was tight.

"What'd you have for breakfast this morning? Faye asked.

"Dry toast and a cup of tea."

"Tomorrow, skip the toast, just tea or coffee."

"Ugh. I'm sorry! I've been so careful."

"Let's try again. Suck in as hard as you can, come on, deep breath." I sucked in even harder, and she magically got it to zip. The last thing I needed was for my dress to rip in the middle of the most important performance of my life.

"Thank you, Faye. You're a lifesaver."

"Anytime. You look swell, dear. Now put some more lipstick on, a little more rouge on your cheeks, and get out there."

I looked in the mirror, reapplied my All-Day Rich and Rosy Lipstick, and dabbed some more rouge on my cheeks. I did look a little pale. My nerves were pretty shaky, but I could always overcompensate with more makeup and accessories. I put on my black satin peep-toe heels and started walking to the stage.

"Audrey! You're up." I heard the Director yelling from the house.

I picked up my pace and walked onstage to the piano. Slowly I sat down as gracefully as I could in the gown and heels and started to play and sing, trying to ignore the butterflies in my stomach that were flitting and twirling around. Was it my nerves, or was it nausea? I wasn't sure why I was so nervous. I had been doing this my whole life, but for some reason, it felt like I was going to be sick on the stage. I tried to shake it off as the music started, and I had only let out a few notes before I needed to stop.

"I'm sorry! I think I'm going to be sick."

I hiked up my dress with both hands so I didn't trip and ran offstage. I luckily found a trash can just in time and threw up into it. Mortified, I prayed I didn't get anything on my dress. I could see Faye thinking the same thing as she flew over to me with a towel and a glass of water, examining the dress.

"Thank you," I said.

"The dress is clean. You, however, are not. Come sit down," she said.

"I don't understand where that came from. I feel completely fine otherwise." I gratefully sat and took a sip of the water while Faye put her hand on my forehead to see if I had a fever.

"You don't have a fever. If anything, you feel a little clammy. Have you been nauseous any other time this week?"

"Well, now that you mention it, the other morning I was, but I just figured it was from the Chinese food we ate late the night before that didn't sit well with my stomach."

"Hmm. Do you think you could be pregnant?"

"Pregnant? No, I mean, not now, but I guess… well—"

"Is your monthly late?"

I started calculating in my head. My monthly cycle was always on time, but I'd been so busy in rehearsals, practicing, and then coming home to make dinner for Ted I hadn't been keeping track lately. Thinking about it, I realized I was three months late. I hadn't planned on this. I thought the children would come after the dream, not before, and definitely not during.

I heard Larry, the Director, before I saw him. The man never needed a microphone because he had one volume level: loud.

"What's going on? We can't afford to waste time like this in the middle of dress rehearsal," Larry said.

"I'm so sorry. I was sick." That was all he needed to know. I was sick. People get sick all the time.

"Well, clean yourself up and get back on stage. Stage fright happens—"

"This wasn't stage fright," I said quietly.

"You don't look sick," Larry says.

"I, I…" I was afraid to say it out loud.

"What is it? Spit it out already."

I hadn't even said it out loud to myself yet. It felt strange to be saying it to Larry before Ted, but he pushed me into a corner I couldn't get out of in that moment.

"I think I might be pregnant."

"Oh, stop. You're just being dramatic."

"This isn't something I would dramatize."

"Are you sure?"

"Well, no, not a hundred percent. I'll need to go to a doctor to be sure of that."

"Oh, and we are supposed to just what, sit around and wait when we have a show to put on?"

"You wouldn't have to wait that long, I'll—"

"We can't have a woman in your condition performing onstage!"

"No, no, please, no one has to know. I'll wear a girdle. I can hide it! it will be fine."

"That's ridiculous. You can't hide a baby Audrey. You're fired."

"No! Please don't do this! You don't mean that."

"Just go back to playing a housewife. There is a line of women out the door who can replace you."

A housewife. A mother. Replaceable. I was so angry I could have spit. I was not *just* a housewife, and I for sure was not replaceable. At that moment, he had *all* the power, and I had none. Would he have fired a man if he shared his wife was expecting? Of course not. Somehow carrying a child made me incapable of performing? I didn't lose my voice. I just had another little human growing inside of me. I'd be damned if I let him get the last word in.

"That's where you're wrong. I'm irreplaceable!"

I held my head up high and marched back to my dressing room, took my dress off, and threw it in a pile on the floor. I could care less about that stupid dress and everything it represented at that point. I wiped the rouge and lipstick off my face and put on my slacks and blouse that felt warm and comforting like I was back in my own skin. I scanned my dressing room as I said goodbye to one dream and hello to another.

Mother of the Century

AUDREY
I look around
And all that I see
Is my dream
ripped right from under me
Is this it?
Is this where I'm supposed to be?

Is this all I was made for?
Mother of the Century?
Is this It?
Is this what I have to be?
Is this all that I worked for?
Mother of the Century

That girl on the beach
She dreamed of children
Never knew how young she'd be
I was that girl
Who wanted it all
A career and a family
But that's not reality
I look around
And all that I see
Is my future
this life that's inside of me

So if this is it
If this is where I'm supposed to be
Then I'll work even harder
And everyone will see
I'll be the mother of the century
I'm the mother of the century

As I left the theater and headed home, it seemed like every person on the street was a mother. Some were pushing a child in a stroller, others holding toddlers' hands as they crossed the street, and every shop window I looked in was full of pink and blue baby clothes.

I couldn't name any of the emotions I was feeling. Losing a dream and becoming a mother at the same time had me feeling every emotion, all at once.

I wondered what Ted would think when I told him.

CHAPTER 22

MY THEATER FAMILY

ROSE: ROSE AND OSCAR'S APARTMENT, NEW YORK— 1952

While Audrey had been busy starting a traditional family of her own, my untraditional theater family kept Oscar and me busy.

For decades, our apartment served as a late-night haven for Broadway stars. Oscar would be sitting at the piano playing standards, and the latest Broadway songstresses would gravitate to the music, martinis in hand. Sometimes, the after-show performances were even better than the actual performances themselves.

Cigarette smoke billowed around the living room, and I would constantly refill our friend's drinks, empty ashtrays, and serve hors d'oeuvres. I always knew when the actors hadn't eaten before the show because they ran right to the kitchen asking what I had at the ready. The dears truly sang for their supper. The chorus girls and boys always seemed the hungriest, and their bodies took a toll from dancing their feet off eight times a week.

I was always in awe of the amount of talent just sprinkled across our couch on any random night, but Sundays were the night the parties lasted into the wee hours of the morning. There were no shows on Monday to rest up for.

Oscar had also started expanding his scope of scouting and had begun producing as well. When he had found his first show to produce, I had been a bit skeptical, but Oscar seemed certain it was a good idea.

"I think this show is going to be something special."

"Oscar, don't you think you should stick to scouting?"

"Not with a gem like this without a producer to see it through. I'd be leaving money on the table if I passed this investment up."

So, he invested.

Opening night of this little obscure musical *Wherever You Are*, was an incredibly proud moment for both of us, though. The audience went wild at the curtain call with a standing ovation after standing ovation, and there was a glowing review in paper the next day, an *"Off-Broadway delightful surprise."* The cast, of course, ended up back at our apartment after, and I watched the dynamics of a theater family unfold before my eyes. It reminded me fondly of my days working in the costume shop. A bond happened throughout working on a show, and the cast and crew would become your family. And as with any family, there was bound to be gossip, drama, love, laughter, and tears.

Our two leading actors, Betty, and John were constantly fighting for the spotlight, and the show's Director, Ralph, had to manage two very large egos that both needed validation. I distinctly remembered him lecturing the two of them early on in rehearsals, "You two better not sleep together because if you do, the show is ruined!"

I honestly didn't understand why until during one of the performances mid-run. Throughout the show, they were both tripping over themselves on stage, and all the organic sexual chemistry they'd had previously seemed off. I never judged how cast romances happened, and they always had a way of working out. The actors spent more time with each other than their own families, and to see the way the youngsters would walk into our apartment hand in hand, arm in arm, kissing and hugging, made me smile.

There was a lot of love, and it wasn't always sexual—it was deeper than that. They were brothers and sisters, aunts and uncles, and it filled our apartment with so much noise and love and creativity I thought my heart might burst.

I loved each of them as if they were my own.

I mended their socks when they got a hole in them, I listened at the kitchen table to tale after tale of heartache and the worries of where the next job would come from, I sent them home with left-overs, and sometimes I would put some cash in their pocket for cab fare. I didn't mean to mother them, but I just couldn't help it. They were all in such need of mothering, and I was in need of a family. Oscar was, of course, my family, but this was the family I chose.

It had been years since that night when I saw Oscar and the blond down the hall. It had gone on for about six months or so, and then for a while, Oscar would come sleep in our room for a few months. The cycle went on like this for years. He'd meet some "pet" and take her under his wing. The ones with stars in their eyes always seemed to be his type— talented, driven, but a little bit broken. It would eventually fade. The guilt would riddle him, and then he'd be incredibly devoted to me again. We'd go back to our routines, and each time he'd come back to me, it was a reminder it was me he really loved. No one could replace me. Sure, they could give him what I couldn't or *wouldn't,* but they could not replace his wife.

During the run of *Wherever You Are,* we were in the part of the cycle where he wasn't with anyone else, and I treasured the months when I had his undivided attention like we were partners again. The cast would affectionately refer to us as mom and dad, and we didn't mind because those were our roles to play. They would run in and say to us, "Mom, you are never going to believe what happened backstage tonight!"

And I'd let them vent and share both the good and the bad moments of their night with me and acknowledge how they felt.

They would respond with, "You and Dad listen so much more than our real parents do." That was always nice to hear. Everyone needed someone to listen to them.

Unfortunately, we had a delicate situation a few months into the run. Dean, one of the chorus boys, had shown up to the theater with a black eye and two broken ribs. He had gone out to a bar straight from the theater the night before and was still in full makeup and got beat up on the way to the subway.

Dean didn't have to tell us why he was beat up. We knew why. They took one look at a man in full stage makeup, which threatened their own sexual identity. It rattled the cast, the girls were all crying, and Oscar was so furious he called the cops to report the incident. Afterward, while it seemed over the top to the cast, Oscar hired some "muscle" that would stay close to the theater and would keep eyes out for the cast's safety.

I insisted Dean stay with us while he recovered from his injuries, and I knew Oscar wouldn't protest. Dean was from

Indiana, a long way from home, and all alone. His parents had thrown him out when he was fourteen when they had caught him with a boy from his baseball team.

It made me angry to even think about it. Dean's parents didn't know how lucky they were. Having a child was such a wonderful gift, and to be lucky enough to have a son as talented as Dean only to throw him out like he was nothing more than a stray cat? That just infuriated me. Didn't they know there were people out there dying to have children who would love them no matter what? It made Oscar and me beyond angry, and I think that's why we secretly loved Dean the most.

When the two of them came home that night, I could barely look at them. It broke my heart to see beautiful Dean, with his perfectly smooth, peachy skin, all bruised and broken. But it wasn't just his face and ribs that were bruised and broken. From the look on Oscar's face, it was his spirit too. Oscar looked like he'd aged about ten years in a day, and in that moment, I knew what having a son must feel like. You wanted to protect them from harm, and when they got hurt, you failed.

Oscar was carrying that weight. I could feel it in my chest, too, and had to look away for a moment to collect myself.

"Come on, Dean. Come lay down on the couch to rest. I just finished making some chicken soup, and I'll bring it out to you. Oscar, can you help him get comfortable?"

"Of course, dear. Rest is just what the doctor ordered."

"The soup smells delicious, Mom, thank you, thanks to both of you," Dean groaned, sinking into the couch. He was obviously still in a lot of pain.

"How about a brandy with the soup?" Oscar suggested.

"I think he really needs fluids right now to heal," I said in my best nurselike voice.

"Technically, brandy is a fluid," Dean joked with a small smirk.

"Smart boy." Oscar smiled.

"Glad to see you still have your sense of humor intact. Brandy it is. For you and Oscar." I went over to the bar next to the piano to pour them their drinks, happy I had not one but two family members to take care of that night.

After dinner and a couple of drinks, Dean went to bed in the guest room, and Oscar and I had a moment to process what had happened that night.

We had both collapsed onto the couch when Oscar asked, "Are you all right? You look exhausted."

"I think I know what being a mother must feel like. It's a constant state of worry," I replied. Oscar opened his arms, and I climbed into them for a hug.

He kissed the top of my head and said, "Yes, and a wonderful worrier you are. But you are an even better mother. You are constantly taking care of everyone around you."

"I do enjoy taking care of our theater family. But it feels like there has to be more we can do."

"Well, there is, if you'd be willing to listen."

"What?"

"What if we tried again to have our own?"

"Oh, Oscar. You can't be serious. I'm so old!"

"No, you're not, and I am serious. Audrey is still having children."

"She's five years younger than me and more fertile than Aphrodite herself! I'm sorry, Oscar, but it's too late for us."

"We could try."

"I love you. But no. I can't." I *wouldn't* risk the pain of getting pregnant and losing another child. He knew, and I didn't know why he wouldn't just leave it be.

"I was afraid you would say that." Oscar's warm embrace turned cold as he removed his arms from around me. I could see the shift in his eyes from hope to disappointment. "I'm going out. I'll be back for breakfast with Dean."

And with that, the conversation was over, and Oscar's hope was gone. I thought he was going to propose something philanthropic for children or the theater, not become *actual* parents ourselves at this stage in our lives. Not after everything we had already been through.

I had upset him again. We had been in one of our good moments of the cycle, getting closer, becoming happier together. Why did he have to ruin it all by bringing up children? I wished I could've given him the answer he wanted, but I couldn't, and so my focus went back to Dean and a situation I could control.

Dean stayed with us for a few weeks until his ribs healed, and he was able to get back to the show. Having Dean there filled the apartment with a different energy, and Oscar and I both missed him terribly, insisting he come over for dinner once a week, to which he did not protest. Both his presence and his absence were a bittersweet reminder of what Oscar and I didn't have and how we just kept disappointing each other.

Maybe one day we'd get it right.

CHAPTER 23

BROKEN TEACUPS

———

AUDREY: TED AND AUDREY'S HOUSE, SPRING—1943

Ted and I were slow dancing in the living room as he was trying to cheer me up. He had tried just about everything these past few months to get my mind off of Carnegie. My head was on his chest, and it felt good to be close to him. I closed my eyes and tried to let the music and his warmth soothe me, but my mind was replaying the feeling of being on that stage singing and playing my heart out in a gorgeous red gown, and I wondered what the audience would've done on opening night. Would they have given me a standing ovation? Would my dressing room have been covered in flowers? Would my picture have ended up in the paper the next day? I'd never know.

"I was so close. So close."

"I know," he said.

"I'm not trying to sound ungrateful. I've always wanted to be a mother." I didn't want Ted to feel guilty about this or think I didn't want our child, because of course, I did. I just couldn't believe the timing. Why would God give me my dream and then take it away and replace it with another dream all in the same day? I couldn't make sense of any of it. Why did he give us gifts and then not allow us to use them?

"You're gonna make a great mom," he said and then put his hand affectionately on my belly. "Get off your feet, and I'll get you some more tea." I dutifully sat on the couch as he took my shoes off and gently put my feet up before heading to the kitchen. I was so incredibly lucky to have him, and he was going to make a wonderful father. He already took such good care of me.

I was about to lay my head down on a pillow to rest when I heard a knock at the door. I got up and took my teacup in hand, drinking the last sip on the way to the door. I opened it and dropped my teacup, shattering it on the floor.

"Vic!"

I thought I was dreaming, but it was really him. He walked toward me, and it was like the whole world was in slow motion. We both stood there soaking in each other's faces. I had thought about that moment so many times I couldn't even begin to count. He touched my face gently, and it was like an electric shock shot through me. Every part of my body was shaking and telling me to move toward him, but my brain was fighting with my body, and I needed to resist.

Then he kissed me, and I couldn't stop it.

We were suddenly back on the beach, and I could smell the salty breeze and feel his arms around me. Bobby was waiting for us at the bar, there was no war, and there was no loss, or pain, or men leaving, and women left behind. There was just love, music, and dreams ahead of us. I let myself remember as I kissed him back, wishing and hoping that could all be true again.

"Get your hands off my wife," Ted said, walking toward Vic, ready to punch him. Oh, God. He'd seen us. I had barely been married a year, and I was kissing another man. But how could I not when he had practically come back from the dead?

"Your, what?" Vic stammered.

"You heard me, my wife."

"Audrey?" Vic looked at me confused and betrayed, and I thought my heart might break again right there.

"Vic, I'm sorry." I *was* sorry. I honestly had let go of the idea of him ever coming home.

"Ted, please, give us a minute to talk. Please," I begged and looked into Ted's eyes. They were full of rage and fear. I reached for his hand to try and calm him down, but he squeezed it so hard I was afraid of what would happen if I wasn't right in between him and Vic. I wanted to avoid anyone getting physically hurt that night, as I had already covered emotionally hurting everyone.

"To talk, Audrey, just talk, two minutes," Ted said and headed back to the kitchen in disgust.

I was grateful for his grace in that moment as I knew I didn't deserve it from either of them. I looked at Vic, who was quietly standing in shock, waiting for an explanation.

"Let me explain! I thought you were dead."

"Well, clearly, I am very much alive!"

"I know, but I never thought you would come home, and Bobby was dead, and I was heartbroken!"

Beautiful Music Together

VIC
Every day was like a nightmare
The things I saw I can't unsee
Brothers dying every minute
The streets bleed with cruelty

But when I closed my eyes
And I blocked out the screaming
I heard you
And your music kept me alive
I saw you
And your smile kept me from drowning
I felt you
And I prayed for the day
I'd hold you again
And we'd make beautiful music together

Every day I waited for your letters
I clung to them to fill my dreams
Of you and I together
Melody and Harmony
But when I closed my eyes
And blocked out the screaming

AUDREY & VIC
I heard you
And your music kept me alive
I saw you
And your smile kept me from drowning
I felt you
And I prayed for the day
When I'd hold you again
And we'd make beautiful music together

VIC
I didn't think that I could make it
I was barely holding on
I crawled through sand

I walked through fire
I heard your song
It kept me strong

He walked toward me and embraced me, and I realized it was not just me who needed comforting at that moment. While his arms were so much stronger than mine, it was me who was holding him at that moment. For the nights on the battlefield when I couldn't hold him. I'd never be able to make this right.

"I promised I'd come home—our music. How could you throw that away?" he said softly.

I pulled away, thinking of his decision to enlist a month after Bobby had died. He could have stayed and been here with me in my grief. Bobby had been a brother to him too. That's what he should've done. We wouldn't have been in this horrible situation if he had just stayed!

"You left me."

"No, you left me. I wrote you every week," he said angrily.

"I never got a single letter from you! I waited and waited, and nothing!"

"That doesn't make any sense Audrey, what do you mean you never got any letters?"

"It didn't make sense to me either, Vic, but I swear I never got them. Please forgive me! I love you!" I tried to comfort him, but he pushed me away.

"Love me?"

"I love you both. Try to understand—"

He interrupted me violently, "I will never understand."

VIC

Now today is a new nightmare
One I never thought I'd see
Betrayal like no other
A vice that won't let me free
But when I closed my eyes
And I blocked out the screaming
I heard you
And your music kept me alive
I saw you
And your smile kept me from drowning
I felt you
And I prayed for the day
I'd hold you again
And we'd make beautiful music...

His voice was still the most gorgeous sound I'd ever heard as it pierced through my heart. I didn't think that moment could get any more confusing and painful until he addressed the elephant in the room as he glanced down at my belly.

"Audrey, is it mine?" he asked quietly.

I shook my head. "No."

He looked as if I had just punched him in the gut. That was the final blow—the final blow to his ego, to our love, to our future. I could see it all over his face. There was no coming back from this. He took off the gold cross I'd given him and dropped it on the piano.

"Goodbye, Audrey."

He walked out of the house, slamming the door behind him. My God, what had I done? Was it possible for three hearts to be broken in one night?

Thankfully, Ted gave me my space, and we didn't say a word to each other that night. He didn't ask what Vic and I discussed, and I didn't have it in me to tell him either. We recovered, slowly, and had the joy of our first child to look forward to in the coming months, but there would always be the memory of Vic returning lingering between Ted and me.

I knelt down and started to pick up the pieces of the broken teacup that had shattered all over the floor and nicked myself on the sharp edges. As blood dripped onto the china, I was thankful for the pain; a reminder of the pain I had caused these two men I loved and the consequences I would have to live with.

CHAPTER 24

BLEND INTO
THE BACKGROUND

"Oh. My. God. Grandma, that is so, so sad. Romantic, but sad, like heartbreaking romantic sad," Amelia says after I finish.

"Yes, it was, and it still is. Reliving these memories is not easy, nor are they memories I'd share if your grandfather were still alive," I say. That wouldn't be fair to Ted.

"So, then what happened? Did you ever see Vic again?" she asks, eyes wide like she's waiting to find out how a romantic movie ends.

"I had a lot of your aunts and uncles, including your mom, is what happened next." I don't answer her about Vic. I'm not ready yet.

My first pregnancy with my daughter Helen was joyful and complicated, though I knew having her was a choice I'd never regret. She was the easiest baby; gentle, snugly, and sweet. She even slept through the night. But I couldn't help but play the what-if game. What if I had her just two years later? What if I hadn't gotten pregnant right out of the gate? How would my life be different now?

"Right, a baby every year," Amelia says.

Robbie came right after Helen, and we named him after my brother. He had his eyes, and if a baby could be born with charisma, he was, just like his namesake. Bernadette came after Robbie, and then the rest well, they just kept coming, one year after the next. Motherhood was all-encompassing, fun, exhausting, and somewhere along the line, I just didn't have time for performing outside of playing my piano after dinner each night. I missed it terribly, but how could I do it with thirteen children to care for?

We all had to make sacrifices to support our family, myself included, even if it meant sacrificing a part of myself.

AUDREY AND TED'S HOUSE, FALL—1958

I had sat down at the piano and started playing some Patsy Cline, hoping it would put Ted in a good mood. We both needed a distraction from the bills we needed to pay, and this baby loved it when I played the piano. I could feel him or her kicking along to the beat, much to the detriment of my ribcage.

I had a stiff drink waiting for Ted in the living room when he came in while I played and sang "I'll Go Walking After Midnight." He had sat down on the floral couch to the left of the piano, relaxing, drink in hand, and a few bars into the song, he began tapping his foot in time with the blues beat and humming along. Mission accomplished. He was smiling, and he *never* smiled at the end of the month. Ted took a big sip of his whisky, and when I'd finished playing, we headed to the kitchen together.

Having already fed and bathed the younger children, the older ones were out with their friends or upstairs playing their rock and roll on the record player. That night was exceptionally quiet, which was a rare occurrence in our usually bustling household.

The white wallpaper in the kitchen, covered with the lemons, oranges, and pickle jars, was so faded and stained the white of it had turned to yellow. I remembered thinking it was cute when we moved in, all bright, white, and sunny. Now, I could barely look at it without seeing something broken or dirty. I could still even see that one spot where one of the babies threw spaghetti sauce at the wall that never came off. The avocado green refrigerator, which was the only thing updated in the kitchen, had a door that got stuck every time you closed it and leaked something awful. The white cabinets with the red trim were barely holding on for dear life from all the slamming of doors, kids playing inside them, and just the wear and tear of eighteen years feeding a family of fifteen.

God, I hated that kitchen.

I pulled a kitchen chair out and sat down slowly. I could barely see the table. There were so many bills stacked on it, but at least it was covering up the table, so I didn't have to look at all the scratches and stains from years of art projects, homework, and spilled milk.

"Where's the electric bill?" Ted asked as he rummaged through the piles. I helped sort through and grabbed an envelope.

"In this pile," I said. Ted took the envelope and put it in another pile. So much for Patsy Cline warming him up. His happy mood had turned sour, just like the milk in the fridge.

"It goes in this pile," Ted said.

"That's the pile we're going to pay this week," I said.

"That's right. You want our electricity turned off?" Ted asked.

'Well, it wouldn't be the first time,' I had thought, but that wouldn't be helpful. I looked at the checkbook and realized we couldn't pay the electric bill without bouncing a check. "We won't have the money till next week," I said.

Ted had studied to get his real estate license that year, and it made a big difference in the summers when he wasn't getting paid. He always found a way for us to get by, worked harder than anyone I knew, and thankfully he had sold a house last month. However, his commission check hadn't come in yet.

"Take it from the grocery budget," Ted said.

"If we keep taking from the grocery budget, we won't have any food. We barely have enough food to begin with. I'm fine with being the last to eat or skipping meals altogether, but with this little one on the way, I can't skip meals, and I am not fine with my kids not having enough."

"It will have to be pancakes for dinner again… or the kids and I will fast." God help me if I had to make or eat another pancake.

"For a week?" Ted put his head in his hands, and I wished I could make it better. There was so much pressure on him to provide. I put my hand on his back to comfort him when I saw a bigger envelope we hadn't gotten to with St. Elizabeth University stamped on the front, my alma mater.

I picked up the envelope and showed it to Ted. "It's a letter from St. E's. Should I open it?"

"I'm sure they are just asking for a donation, but yeah, open it."

"St. Elizabeth's is proud to accept you... into teacher's college!"

"Oh my God. Helen got in!"

"Of course, she did!" We both took in the weight of that news. Ted's face dropped from pride to utter panic just as I had the same thought. How would we pay for it?

"We have to tell her."

"Yes, we do, but Audrey, you know we—"

"Nope, we are not going to ruin this moment for her by talking about money Ted."

"Okay, but we are going to *have* to talk about money."

"I know, but let's tell her the good news first." I walked out of the kitchen to the bottom of the hallway stairs and yelled to Helen to come down to the kitchen.

She came down the stairs with a book in her hand. "What is it, mom?"

"Can you come into the kitchen, please? Your father and I have something to show you."

"Okay... what?"

"Just, come sit down." Helen sat down at the kitchen table next to Ted and looked at us impatiently, flipping through her book. Ted handed her the letter.

"This came for you. We didn't realize what it was."

Helen tore open the envelope, and she read the letter to us. "St. Elizabeth's is proud to accept you into teacher's college! I got in!"

"Of course, you did! You're a girl, you're Irish, you can do anything," I said and planted a big kiss on her cheek. She wiped my lipstick off as Ted stood and hugged her, and then I climbed into hug Ted. The three of us all wrapped up together just like how Ted and I used to dance with her in between us as a baby.

Where had eighteen years gone? How was my baby already a young lady ready to go off to college?

"We are so proud of you, Helen," Ted said. I knew he was. As educators, we always took the education of our children very seriously.

"I have to tell the others," Helen said, yelling to her younger sisters. "Bernadette, Veronica..." and she ran out of the room as fast as she'd run in. Ted and I sat back down to process the news further.

"Our first daughter going to college, and a Catholic college just like her mother," I said.

"Audrey, we can't." Ted shook his head and looked sick to his stomach. "I don't know how we're going to pay for this."

"Maybe it's about time I go back to work," I said.

"Two teachers' salaries aren't going to be enough," Ted replied.

"I will not rob my daughter of the opportunity of higher education." I wondered if Ted would be saying the same thing if it had been Robert, our oldest son. There was always a way, always.

"So, you're going to rob the younger ones of food?" Ted asked. Of course, I wasn't, but he was right. Even if I went back to teaching, we would still be short every month.

I didn't want the rest of the kids to suffer for the gain of one. That wouldn't be fair. My eyes wandered, trying to think of a solution, and then the light bulb went off. I could see it out of the corner of my eye in the living room. The beautiful piano I'd had since childhood. The piano I had been determined to learn how to play and taught myself on. The piano Bobby and I carved our initials into as little kids with big dreams and stars in our eyes.

"How much do you think we could sell the piano for?" I asked.

"What?" Ted asked.

"The piano."

"Audrey, no, you can't," Ted said. I ignored him and walked into the living room. Sitting down on the piano bench, I placed my fingers on the keys.

Blend into the Background

AUDREY
How did I get here?
There has to be a way

I can't blend into the background
I can't dull the light that's within
always felt a little different
wasn't sure where to fit in
I don't follow the rules I've been given
don't know how to do things small
I can't blend into the background
Not when I can hear the call

Music is the language I speak
Children are the gifts from above
I gave up one dream for the other
music is what I can give to the one I love

I've always been a little selfish
always been a little proud
pushed our life to the limit
It's hard to hear when I say it out loud
I won't blend into the background
I won't stick my head in the sand

I won't ignore the dreams of our children
I won't sit still; I'll give them all I can

I gave up one dream for the other
I have nothing left to give as a mother

Helen came running back into the living room and handed me her letter.

"Mom! It says the check is due on the fifteenth," she said.

Music is the air I breathe
How can I give up the air?
I'd give up anything for you
there is nothing I wouldn't do

She won't blend into the background
She'll shine through and make us proud
These are the keys to her future

I longingly traced my fingers over the piano one more time and knew what I had to do. I got up from the piano, walked back into the kitchen, opened the junk drawer, and got out the phone book. I thumbed through it to find the number I needed, and then I walked over to the phone and dialed the number.

"Hello, yes, is this the antique piano shop on seventy-third street? I have a Steinway baby grand from the 1930s, and I'd like to look into selling it."

"Audrey, hang up the phone. We'll—" Ted came up behind me.

"Shh…" I said as I waved my hand at him. Helen needed to go to college, and I was not going to get in the way of that.

I had strong faith God would provide what we needed. He would give and take away, but he always provided a way out.

"Audrey, we will find another way. I'll sell more houses. We can sell the car!" Ted suggested, his eyes pleading with me to stop talking to the piano shop, but I was not hanging up.

"How would you get to work?" I mouthed back. "There is no other way, Ted. This *is* the way. I have to do this." Selling my piano was like selling a part of myself. I could feel the parts of me I loved fading away, and yet I would do it all over again if it meant providing for my children.

Little did I know just how many parts of myself I would be losing. My piano was the first.

CHAPTER 25

WHO'S THE BABY?

———

AUDREY: AUDREY AND TED'S HOUSE, CHRISTMAS EVE—1958

I took a quick peek in the bathroom mirror, and raccoon eyes stared back at me. I reapplied my All-Day Rich and Rosy Lipstick and powdered under my eyes to cover the dark mascara mixed with tears. I took a sip of water and walked back into the living room and put on my best smile.

"Mom, are you all right?" Veronica asked, looking concerned.

"I'm fine. Don't worry about me. I always get a little sentimental at Christmas," I replied soothingly.

I couldn't help it if the emotions came out. Being a mom was really, really hard. But that year had been especially hard because we had sold the piano. That was why I was really crying. Money was always tight, but I tried to make Christmas special for each of my children. I know people joked and said I was like a baby factory, and I guess I kind of was, but with each baby, I felt like I was bringing a new song into the world; twelve, soon to be thirteen, songs altogether.

Music was always at the heart of every holiday in our house. One of my favorite family traditions was how we spent

Christmas Eve. It was chaos getting all the kids dressed in their best clothes, and I often leaned on the older ones to dress the younger ones. That year, like many others, Rose showed up with bags and bags of beautiful red and green velvet dresses for the girls and matching bowties and crisp button-downs for the boys. As usual, there was complaining from the boys their clothes were itchy, but the girls always loved the holidays when they could dress up and not be in their school uniforms. I didn't want to know what Rose spent on the clothes she brought, and yet I was sure for her and Oscar it was nothing.

Rose and Oscar were a vision of Christmas elegance and looked out of place in our cramped and chaotic living room. Oscar had his hand on the small of Rose's back ever so protectively, while Rose's fingers balanced her wine glass perfectly while holding one of the babies on her lap. Her emerald, green dress made her waist look as tiny as possible, and I remember being very conscious of my own thickening waist. Ted was in his best black suit and dark green tie and walked out of the kitchen with a cup of tea for me and two shots of whisky for him and Oscar.

"You looked like you could use this," Ted said sweetly and kissed me on the top of my head. I thankfully took a sip, hoping it would calm the nausea. I hugged him and whispered into his ear, "Thank you."

"Merry Christmas!" Ted said and handed Oscar a shot with exuberance.

"What are we drinking to?" Oscar asked curiously.

"To number thirteen on the way!" Ted said with pride, looking at me. "All I have to do is look at Audrey, and she gets—"

"Ted! Shhh… the children don't know yet," I said tensely and felt myself blushing.

"We are among family, Audrey. It's okay. The kids are so distracted they can't hear a thing anyway," Ted said, calming me down.

"Well, it's wonderful news. We are so happy for you both, aren't we, Oscar?" Rose said, smiling.

"Of course!" He lowered his voice and whispered, "To number thirteen!" and then he and Ted both threw back their whisky.

I could sense some unfinished business between Rose and Oscar. I tried to be sensitive to our ever-growing family and the fact they didn't have one, but something seemed different with them tonight.

Ted was right. The kids hadn't heard a thing. They were so distracted and excited for Christmas. There were children everywhere. Robert and Veronica, two of my older children, were sitting on the stairs with a pile of pots, wooden spoons, and soup ladles from the kitchen next to them. They were clearly conspiring something for the evening's show. Helen, the oldest, was helping the little one's string popcorn to make garlands, and as each popcorn kernel got strung on one end, Meredith and Jane were eating them off the other end giggling uncontrollably. Their innocent and joyful little laughs put a huge smile on my face. They were the spirit of Christmas.

The sweetness of the girl's laughter was interrupted by a loud "Ow, why'd you do that?" as Daniel and Patrick, six and seven years old respectively, were snapping each other's suspenders. Somehow, Patrick had taken one of his straps off and snapped Daniel right in the eye. It looked a little red, but he'd be fine. If we could avoid an emergency room visit on Christmas Eve, it would be a win.

Bernadette had a scowl on her face as two little ones attempted to braid her hair. She would have rather been upstairs reading or listening to a record than playing dress-up with the little ones. It was hard being a teenager with eleven brothers and sisters. She had so much more responsibility than a normal teenage girl should have. In a way, Bernadette and Helen were both second mothers to their younger siblings, and I could see how that weighed on Bernadette.

The living room, while filled with noise, felt stark. I missed my piano, but I'd be damned if I let the kids see that. "Take your seats! It's time for the annual Christmas Eve show to begin. Now you all know the rules. Everyone must perform something," I said.

The younger children stopped what they were doing and dutifully lined up in the center of the living room and sat on the floor. Robert handed them each a pot, a wooden spoon, and a ladle. They had the percussion section handled. Helen and Veronica ran over to the adults and placed the garlands of popcorn and holly around our necks. Bernadette was visibly annoyed and too cool for all of it, but she placated her sisters, and the three formed a semicircle and began to sing.

HELEN/BERNADETTE/VERONICA
Deck the halls with boughs of holly
Fa la la la la, la la la la (fa la la la la, la la la la)
'Tis the season to be jolly

Robert made a grand entrance wearing a Santa suit and holding a big red bag. He put his hands on his belly, letting out a big laugh. He looked adorable. The Santa suit was enormous on him, and he was skinny as a rail, as all the kids were, and it was a sight to behold! Ted winked at me, and we couldn't help but chuckle to ourselves.

"HO-HO-HO!" Robert bellowed.

HELEN/BERNADETTE/VERONICA/ROBERT
Fa la la la la, la la la la (fa la la la la, la la la la)

Rose, Oscar, Ted, and I all clapped with vigor, thinking that was the end of the song, but Santa, or Robert, said, "We're tired of that old fa la la la! Let's shake things up a little bit!" He wheeled in a red wagon with the four youngest children. Jane held the baby, Ryan, while Alice was holding a baby doll. Helen, Veronica, and Bernadette each picked up a baby, diapered, swaddled, bottled, and repeated.

Who's the Baby?

HELEN
Who's the Baby
This year?

HELEN/VERONICA
Tell us mama
What's that we hear?
We hear a baby

HELEN/VERONICA/BERNADETTE
Wah Wah Wah Wah

Helen was all smiles as she grabbed a baby out of the wagon, diapered it, swaddled it, gave it a bottle, and passed it down to Veronica, who passed it down to Bernadette. It reminded me how musical they all were and how performing was in their blood. I was so proud of them.

Daniel and Patrick kept filling the wagon with more baby dolls, and Helen, Veronica, and Bernadette couldn't keep up. Helen ran over, picked up another doll, and repeated the process. As soon as she did, another baby doll appeared. Helen, Veronica, and Bernadette were all rocking and pretending to feed the dolls as they swayed to the do-op beat of the song, just like the Supremes. All that was missing were the standing microphones.

HELEN/VERONICA/BERNADETTE
We hear a baby
Wah Wah Wah Wah

Daniel and Patrick pinched baby Ryan, and he started crying right on cue. Robert took center stage, plugged his ears, and handed Ryan to Helen to soothe.

ROBERT

I woke up this morning
To another baby cryin
All I wanted was some cereal
But the milks all gone, and I
Asked my mamma
What's for dinner tonight?
She said, check the freezer
But the meats all gone so
We get pancakes for dinner

Veronica, Helen, and Bernadette are each holding a bowl and pretending to mix pancake batter with spoons. The spoons also served as the perfect fake microphones.

ROBERT/VERONICA/HELEN/BERNADETTE
We got nothing to eat but pancakes for dinner

HELEN/VERONICA/BERNADETTE
Oh Mama
What have you done?
Please no more diapers
They're no fun

Bernadette, holding a baby in one hand, picked up a trash bag full of diapers and tried to hold her nose before throwing it out with a gagging face. Veronica then took a pillow from the couch and put it under her shirt and waddled into the center of the living room pretending to be a pregnant me.

"Mom, another baby? Why do we have so many babies in this house?" whined Bernadette.

Robert then walked in wearing glasses pretending to be Ted. "Well, besides the fact that all I have to do is look at your mom, and she gets..." Robert said, laughing.

"Eww, gross, dad," whined Bernadette cutting him off. "When are you going to stop?"

"Well, Bernadette, who would you rather I didn't have?" Veronica said clearly, mimicking me. That was the answer I gave every time we shared with the kids another baby was on the way. Bernadette rolled her eyes at Veronica.

"Every child is a blessing, and we have been blessed many, many times," Veronica said and then crossed herself.

I knew they were making light of our family situation and of me, the baby-making machine. It was laughable, really. I did always say that as I smiled to myself. But deep down, I heard their resentment. Resentment of how many kids there were and how I had to share the caretaker responsibility with the whole family. They all were parents to each other. How could two parents do it all without help?

"A few too many times, mom!" Bernadette piped back sarcastically.

"I love all the babies!" Helen said energetically.

"Shut up, Helen!" the kids yelled back.

VERONICA/HELEN
Tell us mama
What's that we hear?
We hear a baby

HELEN/VERONICA/BERNADETTE
Wah Wah Wah Wah
We hear a baby
Wah Wah Wah Wah

BERNADETTE
Another baby
Wah Wah Wah Wah

VERONICA
Another baby!
Wah Wah Wah Wah

HELEN/VERONICA/BERNADETTE
Another baby.

We all jumped to our feet and gave the kids a standing ovation, clapping with exuberance.

"Bravo!" Ted cheered. He looked at me, eyes misty, and I didn't know if those were tears of pride or from laughing so hard. I was proud of them, too, of their talent and their sense of humor. I knew with every joke there was a layer of truth, and I couldn't help but be a little sad about that. I wouldn't let them see that, though. Nothing but pride on Christmas.

"Oh, my goodness. That was one of the best Christmas Eve shows yet! I'm so proud of you! Without my piano, I didn't know how we would have a show this year," I said to the children.

"The show must go on! We can make music with anything!" declared Veronica.

"That's right, V. You are never too..."

"...old and you are never too young to make music. I know. I know."

Hearing my own words reflected back to me from my daughter hit me like a punch to the gut. I felt tears welling up, and my chest got tight. I had to walk out of the room to compose myself.

"What? What'd I say?" Veronica asked as I abruptly walked into the hallway. Rose followed me.

"I am too old... I don't even take my own advice," I said to Rose.

"You are not old, and that performance was better than any night at Carnegie Hall could have ever been. Every single one of them has music in their genes, and that's because of you."

"I know they're talented, and believe me, it makes me so proud, but that's not it, Rose. I never got to Carnegie."

"Well, you did... you just..."

"Ugh... don't remind me."

"I'm sorry. I know it's a painful memory. But it's Christmas! There's no crying tonight unless they are happy tears! Besides, we have a surprise for the kids, and I think it might cheer you up. Let's go back and get some food in you."

"You're right—no feeling sorry for myself on Christmas. I have so much to be thankful for. Including you." I had a house full of healthy children, a husband who loved me and worked harder than anyone, and the dearest friend I could ever ask for. The tears started to well again.

"None of that. I'm thankful for you too. Now go fix your makeup. Your mascara is running down your face, and you could use some more lipstick."

"And there's the truth when I need it. I'll be right there." I walked back into the living room after freshening up just as Oscar was gathering the kids.

"Now, kids, Aunt Rose and Uncle Oscar have a surprise for you," he shared with a wink.

"What? What is it?" the kids yelled, jumping up and down with excitement.

"We got tickets to take all of you to your first Broadway show!" Rose said.

The oldest children mouthed "Yes!" to each other, their smiles wide as the younger ones jumped up and down with squeals of pure joy.

"We can't thank you enough," Ted said and put his hand out, and shook Oscar's hand.

"Theater tickets are the most wonderful gift!" I said to Rose and Oscar.

"Our pleasure, Merry Christmas!" they replied. Oscar had his arm around Rose and squeezed her tight. She looked at him with such happiness in her eyes.

"Kids, we have some other news to share with you all," I said, knowing it was time to share the news.

"What is it?" Veronica asked, looking concerned.

"Well, it's kinda funny, like the song you all sang... Ted... do you want to...?" I looked to him for support.

"We are having another baby!" Ted said with pride. The older kids' faces all dropped, Bernadette rolled her eyes. Robert and Veronica both looked at each other with polite grins on their faces, and Helen ran over and gave me a big hug. God bless Helen.

"That's wonderful. I can't wait to meet our newest addition," Helen said and then went to help Jane and Meredith with their toys.

"Great, another baby," Bernadette said. I tried to brush off Bernadette's reaction, and the grumbling in my stomach gave me an idea.

"Hey, who's hungry? Because I'm suddenly craving pancakes. Why don't I go whip some up? With lots of butter and syrup?"

"I'm not hungry," Bernadette said as she walked away.

"Me either," Robert and Veronica chimed in. Defeated, I headed into the kitchen to make a batch just for me.

After stacking my personal batch of pancakes onto a plate, I slathered some butter on them and took a bite as the syrup and butter melted in my mouth. As I swallowed, I felt a little flutter in my stomach and let out a cry. It's okay little one. You will be loved. You already are.

Just then, the door to the kitchen creaked open, and Ted and Rose were standing there. "We heard there were pancakes on the menu tonight. "Ted asked. I burst into tears and laughter all at the same time, reminded I wasn't alone. Rose and Ted were always there when I needed them.

CHAPTER 26

IN HER SHOES

———

Rose has always been a constant in my life. The funny thing about friendship over the decades is how it can ebb and flow, just like fashion. Some styles change, but at the core of every woman's closet are those timeless staples that remain the same and true to form. A simple black dress, a crisp white button-down blouse, your most comfortable pair of flats, a pair of pearl earrings, and the heels that make your legs look fantastic (but also give you blisters if you wear them too long).

AUDREY: NEW YORK CITY, SUMMER—1960

The simple black dress hung in my closet next to my cranberry red house dress. It faded over the years and started to look more like a pale pink, as I had bleached it so much trying to get milk stains and pancake batter out. I couldn't help but think Rose and I were like those two dresses. She was elegant and classy, and I was loud and a little worn out.

While my clothes might have desperately needed updating, the one thing I was never without was my lipstick. Regardless of how much or little was in our bank account or my closet, I had my All-Day Rich and Rosy Lipstick on. It was the one accessory that always made me feel put together, even if I didn't feel like it on the outside or the inside, for that matter.

Rose didn't need lipstick to do that for her.

It was the 1960s, and while some of my daughters were burning their bras, marching on Washington, and sporting bell-bottom jeans, Rose and I were living in our own vastly different realities at this point. On this particular day, she had invited me to an afternoon of shopping and lunch at the Plaza Hotel. I treasured my time with Rose, especially as my family continued to grow. Time away from my children with my best friend was precious. It gave me fuel and a much-needed escape.

Our life trajectories could not have been more different.

I thought of how Rose lived and how different it was from my life. She spent her time entertaining, planning, and hosting dinner parties, shopping for a new dress, and seeing the latest shows with Oscar. I could just imagine what she'd say about her life while I was here changing diapers in the nursery, folding countless loads of laundry, and attempting to cook dinner for fifteen every night.

In Her Shoes

ROSE
Central Park West is my address
the theater is where you'll find me
dressed to the nines all is well all is fine
So what is that voice inside me?
It whispers
You have a husband who loves you
But no, I don't have children
No, I don't have a child
Isn't that wild?

AUDREY

High field lane is my address
the nursery is where you'll find me
in the same dress all the time, all is fine
So what is that voice inside me?
It whispers
You have thirteen children
but my life isn't grand
not a little bit rich
Isn't that rich?

I headed into Saks on Fifth Avenue, and I could see Rose through the store window. She looked like someone who belonged on Fifth Avenue with her perfectly manicured nails, pointing to a pair of gold heels, and her raspberry pink suit, tailored to fit her slender frame like a glove. She looked so incredibly classy that one could assume she would be having lunch with Jackie O herself. How were we related? How did she end up here, living in the center of the theater world in New York City, and I found myself stuck in Nutley?

I hated myself for being jealous at that moment because Rose was so kind and generous to me, but I would be lying to say I wasn't.

I walked into Saks, and Rose's face lit up as she grabbed my hands and kissed me on both cheeks. Ever the graceful hostess, she somehow knew all the salesclerks, and someone handed me a glass of champagne almost immediately. This kind of afternoon was perfect for me! As we walked around the floor, I eyed a beautiful pair of mustang blue heels.

"I'm so glad you could scoot away this afternoon!" said Rose.

"Me too. Thank you for the invitation."

"Now, tell me everything. How are the babies?"

"Mary-Catherine is the sweetest thing. Still so tiny at four months old. She has a very calm demeanor, but she hasn't been sleeping through the night yet, so you could say I'm a bit tired." Tired was an understatement. I hadn't slept more than five hours a night in over a decade.

"Well, of course, you are! I don't know how you do it all, Audrey. And how is little Ryan? Is he a year old now?" she asked, her face scrunching up as if she just saw the cutest puppy.

"Yes, thirteen months now. He's smart as a whip, too. He learned how to climb out of his crib at ten months, and now he's walking. There is no containing him without the baby gate up at all times. He's also very sweet with Mary-Catherine. Those two are going to be thick as thieves when she catches up with him." I smiled, thinking about my two youngest growing up together, knowing Ryan would always look out for her, just as Bobby had looked out for me.

"I'm sure she'll catch up faster than he thinks if she's anything like the rest of the girls in our family," Rose said, letting out a little laugh.

"Exactly. There is no such thing as a weak woman in this family," I said with pride. "Now enough about the babies and me, tell me about New York! How's Oscar? What shows have you seen lately?"

"Oscar is as busy as ever. A few months ago, we saw this little show Off-Broadway, and quite frankly, the first act was dragging. But you know me, I insisted we stay through to the end, and thank goodness we did. There was this actress in the second act, and I tell you, she moved us both to tears."

"Good for her. Did Oscar end up signing her?" I asked, curious about the path of a woman in theater following her dream. I could feel the itch, and the pain, of a dream I had yet to achieve gnawing at me. Sometimes when I had played my piano at the end of a long day, I'd close my eyes and imagine I was on a stage. The living room transformed into a set, and the children magically turned into adoring fans sitting out in the audience.

"He did sign her. She was thrilled," Rose said.

"Your patience and influence have clearly helped him over the years with discovering new talent!" I said, encouraging the role she'd played in Oscar's success. I could see her fiddling with her ring, something she did whenever she was nervous, and her expression looked pained rather than thankful. I wondered what that was about.

"Thank you, Audrey. I'm thankful he listens to my opinions." She smiled and let out a sigh. "That's more than I can say for most men when their wives try to influence their business decisions with their opinions." She tilted her head slightly to the side and raised her eyebrows at me.

"We are full of opinions, aren't we?" I laughed.

"That we are! Oh! Remember that one actress I told you about a year ago, the one with the great comedic timing Oscar knew had so much potential?"

"Sure, I remember you telling me how the two of you could not stop laughing that night," I said.

"Well, she's really starting to make a name for herself. She made her Broadway debut in *Once Upon a Mattress* back in 1959, and now she's breaking into television. You might have seen her on *The Gary Moore Show*," Rose says as if knowing a famous actress was nothing.

Putting two and two together, I asked, "Wait a minute. Are you talking about Carol Burnett?"

"Yes! She's become a dear friend, and Oscar and I just adore her," Rose said, glowing with an almost maternal pride I recognized well.

"Wow," was all I could say in response.

I walked down the aisles of the department store looking at all the luxury brands and fashion I'd never be able to afford, while Rose looked over at the children's clothing section. We were both feeling the extreme contrast of our lives, and with a mix of jealousy, curiosity, and admiration for each other, we started to sing.

ROSE/ AUDREY
What would I give
Just for a day
To walk in her shoes
I'd give it all away
Can I try them on for size?
Would my life be a lie?
To walk in her shoes
I'd give it all way

ROSE/AUDREY
We each made a choice
We followed our voice
it sure looks different
from over here
We must live with our choice
and follow our voice
and quiet our fears
What would I give
just for a day
to walk in her shoes
Would you give it all away?

Of course, I loved my crazy brood of thirteen, but it sure was tempting to daydream of swapping lives with Rose for a day. She handed me the pair of mustang blue heels she saw me eyeing earlier, and I tried them on. They fit perfectly but buying them was not a luxury I could afford or even think of entertaining.

As if reading my mind, Rose said, "These will look divine on you! Excuse me!" She motioned to the salesclerk. "We'll take these in size six and bring the dress and the bag that match." She turned back to me with a bright smile. "This is my treat, Audrey," Rose said, waving her pretend magic wand as my fairy godmother for the day.

"Oh Rose, you know I can never repay you for this."

"Oh yes, you can. Why don't we just pretend to switch lives tonight? Let Oscar and I babysit those beautiful children while you take our tickets to Carnegie Hall."

"Tickets to Carnegie Hall and free babysitting are two things I can't say no to," I blurted out excitedly. It had been almost twenty years since I'd been to Carnegie Hall. There were a lot of mixed emotions flooding through me as I remembered the last time I was there, under very different circumstances.

"It's settled then! Tonight, you can live in my world, front row center at Carnegie Hall."

"And you can live in mine surrounded by the chaos of thirteen children! Somehow, I think I'm getting the better deal tonight," I said teasingly. I was so grateful for what Rose had just gifted me and hoped she was up for what an actual night with thirteen kids was like.

"That's funny. I thought I was." Rose smiled wistfully. She raised her flute glass, and I raised mine. "To our different worlds," she said, and we clinked glasses, toasting to the beautiful day we just had and the night that was about to ensue.

CHAPTER 27

WE WERE JUST KIDS

___

AUDREY: LATER THAT EVENING,
CARNEGIE HALL—1960

A night out in the city with Ted, without the kids, was just what the doctor ordered. I admired my mustang blue heels and matching dress Rose had bought me and was feeling like a million bucks. Though I was nervous about being back at Carnegie, as the last time I'd been there was the night I got fired. I didn't know how I would feel being back, and the what-ifs were already running through my brain. What if I hadn't gotten fired?

I tried to prepare myself in the cab ride with Ted. I was prepared for some memories to come flooding back of that day and the emotions that were all mixed together—joy, disappointment, anger, and excitement. I'd had lots of those feelings over the last eighteen years, but what I could not have prepared for was *who* would be performing that night.

As we sat down, I felt myself get a little queasy. I choked it back like I had so many times before and got ready to enjoy the show. The orchestra started playing, and the sound filled the hall with the most amazing acoustics. I closed my eyes and reached for Ted's hand and felt at peace and at home until I heard his voice, Vic's voice; Mr. Butter himself.

His voice soared, and as it soared, Ted's hand started squeezing mine. I pulled my hand away because he was squeezing so hard it hurt. I opened my eyes to look at Ted, and he was fuming. His face was turning red, and he clenched his hands. I wasn't sure if he was angry at me for pulling my hand away or even angrier that Vic was up there performing.

He huffed loudly and said, "What is he doing here?" I was just as surprised as he was, but I would not make a scene in the middle of a concert. I shrugged my shoulders at him, crossed my legs, and looked intently at the stage, avoiding Ted's eyes. Oscar had paid a lot of money for those tickets, and I would not be wasting them, regardless of Ted's comfort level.

I tried to enjoy the rest of the concert. I really did. Vic sounded as wonderful as always and his voice, if it was possible, was even more powerful. It had grown richer with the maturity of life. I had never really thought about how life could impact a singer's voice, but his voice had aged in the best way possible.

His phrasing was effortless. His lower register poured out like a silk dress and was smooth in all the right places. His falsetto was so pure and light it could make any woman in the audience smile and weep, all in the same breath. I had once sung like that. I used to be able to move people like that with my music. Yet there he was, living *my* dream.

After the concert, I made my way to the stage door, much to Ted's chagrin. He was pacing back and forth while I practiced my most diplomatic smile and pleasantries in my head. I didn't know what to say after all this time, but I had to say something.

"What are we doing here?" Ted asked.

"I think we should at least try talking to him," I replied.

"Why are we wasting time here? Let's go eat. I'm starving."

I didn't respond, still lost in my thoughts. "The show was wonderful. Why are we wasting a perfectly good evening waiting outside the stage door? Let's go get a drink," Ted tried again.

"It's been eighteen years," I said as if Ted needed reminding.

"And you still miss him," he bit back at me. Well, I missed him, he was right, but I honestly had been a little too busy raising thirteen kids to be pining over a lost love.

"Don't you?" I replied instead. He had been Ted's friend too, and we had both lost Bobby and Vic in the same year. Two of our best friends. Maybe, just maybe, we could all be friends again.

"Did you know Vic was performing tonight? Is that why Rose gave you the tickets?" Ted accused.

"No! Of course not. How dare you suggest—" Vic walked out the stage door at that moment and was startled to see us.

"Audrey," Vic said.

"Hello, Vic."

"What a surprise. What's it been, twenty years?" Vic asked.

"Eighteen, but who's counting," I said with a smile.

"You look good, Vic," Ted said and offered his hand. Vic didn't shake it. Clearly, the idea of us being friends again was not going to happen.

"Thanks," Vic said to Ted, looking unsure what to make of this situation. "It's nice to see you." Vic turned back to me and looked me right in the eyes. We stood there awkwardly, in a moment of silence that felt like an eternity. I sensed he still actually blamed Ted and not me, though I had thought he'd hate me after all these years. I thought he'd never want to look at me again.

Ted was the one who broke the silence.

"Hey, what a concert! Who would've thought you'd be playing Carnegie Hall one day? You know Audrey almost played here herself before the kids." Dammit, why had Ted shared that?

"Oh. I didn't know," Vic said. I could hear the surprise and pity in his voice. "Congrats on your family. I hear you have twelve at home, is that right?" I wondered if he'd been keeping tabs on us since he knew that.

"Thirteen," I corrected him.

"Seven girls and six boys," Ted said with pride.

"Wow," Vic said, and after a long pause turned to me, "Well, you did always want to be a mother." He reached into his wallet and pulled out a picture of a beautiful wife and two adorable children and held it up for Ted and me to see. They all had his thick black hair. His wife was a tiny little thing and looked like a bird. A little bird he could control and tame.

I had to tell myself to stop, knowing I'd have hated her no matter who she was or what she looked like. Vic had been the man that got away. While my own choices had caused it, I still hated the idea of someone else having him. I used to be so wild and free when I was with him, and now I felt like I was a mother and nothing else. I wondered what our life would've been like together, though I knew I'd never get to find out.

"My wife would never be out like this with the kids at home. A mother's place is with her children," he said.

"Well, isn't it lucky I'm not your wife then?" I couldn't help myself. Two could play at that game.

"Yes. Yes, it is," Vic said. Ted was sweating and giving me a death stare to stop baiting him, but I couldn't let it go. If we were going to go there, then we were going to go there.

"It must be so fulfilling for you to get to pursue your music career *and* have a family when your wife is home taking care of the kids. I didn't have that option," I said.

"You *did* have that option, Audrey," Vic shot back.

"Now, hold on just a minute. You don't get to talk to me like that. I know we made promises to each other, and I broke that promise, but I had just lost Bobby, and you enlisted and left for war. I didn't know how to handle it, and I was scared! I'll never understand why you didn't propose before you left."

"I was scared too. Scared I wouldn't come home, of losing you," he said softly.

"But you made your choice, and I made mine, as hard as it was," I said.

That was the Gods' honest truth. We'd both made choices we had to live with now, as painful and bitter as they still were. I wouldn't have had my kids if I'd waited for Vic. I didn't know who I'd be without them, and I didn't know who they'd be without Ted and me as their parents.

It was uncomfortably silent, and both Vic and Ted were looking like they'd rather be anywhere else in the world.

"Well, we don't want to take up too much of your time. Come on, Ted, let's go…" I was putting an end to this misery.

"I actually have a meeting with a new agent tonight anyway, so goodnight," Vic replied as he turned to leave. He stopped, though, then turned back to me. "Audrey… I hope you're still working on your music. Children or not, your talent is not something you should just throw away."

I wanted to have the last word in that conversation, but as I was about to open my mouth, for once, I was speechless.

After we had parted ways, Ted and I wandered over to a nearby bench, where I sat for a bit as my ankles swelled like they had so many times before. I was trying desperately to keep my composure and process all that was said, but Ted was still pacing, clearly agitated.

"What's wrong?" I asked.

"Wrong? What's wrong?"

We Were Just Kids

TED

I was there, Audrey
I know how you loved him
I know how you looked at him
I just saw it right now
You've never looked at me like that
I swear you've never looked at me like that

"Ted, that's not—" I started, urging him to come sit down next to me on the bench.

AUDREY

We were just kids
We were just kids when we lost Bobby
We were just kids when Vic went away

TED

You were so sure
Sure, he was never coming home
That you and I would be left all alone
Why should we be alone?
So, I was smitten by your charm
And I liked having you on my arm
But I never wanted to hurt him

"Why the heck did you say yes? Why did you pick me over him?" Ted asked, getting back up to start pacing again.

AUDREY

We were just kids when Vic went away
Of course, I loved him
I wrote him every single day
And I prayed he'd come back to me
Please come back to me
But when it mattered to me
When it mattered most
It was you, helping me stand
You were the armor...
With my hand

I slowly stood and walked toward him, singing our song. The song he had sung to me the night he proposed.

With Your Hand

AUDREY

If I only had today
I would spend it with you
Just to see you smile again
And your eyes shine, the way that they do

If I only had today
I would spend it with you
Just to hear You laugh again
Oh, what I'd give to
Laugh all day with you

TED AND AUDREY
We'll live, like tomorrow never comes
We'll love like the war's already won
Here I stand
I'll be the armor

AUDREY
Let me be the armor

TED
I'll be your armor

AUDREY & TED
with your hand...

We started kissing passionately, losing ourselves for a time and forgetting we were still standing in the middle of the Theater District. I didn't know when the right time to tell him was, but it felt as good a time as any in that moment.

"Ted, there's something I have to tell you."

"Yes?" Ted replied, pulling me closer and kissing my neck.

"I'm expecting again."

"Fourteen kids. Well, that's something Vic will never have," he murmured in my ear.

"No, no, he won't," I said softly.

Ted pulled me to him roughly and kissed me hard. The boom of thunder in the distance interrupted us, and we ran for a cab to avoid getting caught in the rain.

CHAPTER 28

IT HAPPENED AGAIN

AUDREY: AUDREY AND TED'S HOUSE, FALL—1960

Ted was so proud when I told him we were having another one. I was afraid how he'd take it, we had so many mouths to feed already, and I had hoped his reaction was not solely fueled by wanting to compete with Vic. Although I didn't know how having fourteen children proved something. Maybe it did to him, but things didn't go the way we had hoped.

I wish I could say it got easier with each loss, but it didn't. It got harder. I wasn't a young mother anymore, and my body was sore, and so was my heart. I had been trying to rest that afternoon, but the sound of the washing machine shaking kept waking me up. I had headed down the stairs slowly, holding onto the railing to switch the load and hoping one of the girls was around to help.

I was about to walk into the laundry room when I heard the kids all talking to Billy from down the street. Normally when Billy was over, there was a lot of laughing and carrying on, but that afternoon you could practically hear a pin drop. The kids were whispering, but I could make out Robbie, Veronica, Bernadette, and Helen's voices from the next room.

"So, what happened last week, Robbie? I saw you running like a bear was chasing you," Billy said.

"You tell him, Veronica," Robbie said.

"I don't know where to start," Veronica replied.

"How about at the beginning. When did you get home?" Robbie said.

"Okay, um… around three-thirty in the afternoon. I had just gotten home from school, and I couldn't wait to get out of my itchy uniform. I was about to go upstairs, but that's when I saw there was… uh—" Veronica stopped herself.

"What did you see? Spit it out?" Billy asked.

"Hey, take it, easy man, she's just a kid," Robbie said.

So was he. They were all just kids. None of them should have had to come home and see what they saw, and it was not like this was the first time. It had happened so many times.

"Blood. There was blood all over the stairs, okay?" Veronica said.

"That's when I heard her scream," Robbie said.

"And I ran upstairs to find you," Veronica added.

Oh, V. She must have been so scared! I didn't love they were sharing all these details with Billy, as our private family loss was none of his business. Nor was it something I would encourage the kids to talk so openly about, but it was clear they needed to talk about it.

"As soon as I saw the blood, I knew it had happened again," Bernadette said in her dry way.

"Whoa. Like how much blood?" Billy asked.

"Relax, Billy. There was a lot, okay. All thirteen kids were home, and when I saw the blood, I knew I had to keep the little ones safe. I didn't know what we were dealing with," Robert said.

Thank goodness Robert had been home. He was a natural-born leader, just like his namesake. Bobby always knew what to do in a crisis too. Oh, how I longed for my brother in that moment to lean on for comfort.

"What did ya think, was there like a murderer upstairs or something?" Billy leaned in and asked.

I hoped they didn't think that! Those poor kids must have been terrified! For them to have had that thought was just so upsetting. I wished I could go back in time and protect them from what they'd seen. I could see how much the older children had matured compared to their friends. They had to grow up faster just due to the sheer size of our family and their responsibilities, and I didn't know if they would ever recover from that.

"There could've been, I didn't know what had happened, but I knew it wasn't good. I told the big kids to take the little ones down to the basement as fast as they could," said Robert.

"I was scared. I thought someone was in the house, like a robber, or a … a… worse than that. I didn't know what to do," Veronica admitted.

"I could hear mom crying upstairs. I didn't know if she was hurt or sick, but I had to do something. I told Helen and Bernadette to stay with the little ones, climbed through the basement window, and ran as fast as I could to Dr. O'Connor's house." Robert said.

I hadn't known that. How incredibly brave Robbie had been. I just remembered laying on the bathroom floor and Dr. O'Connor knocking on the door and magically being there when I needed him. I'd been in so much pain I hadn't even asked how he'd known to come. Now I knew. My teenage son and Dr. O had saved my life.

"Ahh, that's when I saw you running. He's a good guy that Doc," Billy said.

"He is," Robert replied. "I was very thankful he was home when we needed him."

"So what were you girls all doing while Robbie was chasing to get Dr. O?" Billy asked.

"I told the little ones everything was going to be fine," Helen explained, "but I knew it wasn't fine. My mind kept racing to the worst-case scenario. I told the others not to worry about mom, she was just upstairs taking a little rest, and then I put some music on and started playing chutes and ladders to pass the time."

God bless Helen. She took her role as the oldest sister so seriously and was wonderful with her younger brothers and sisters. I had never intended on her having to be like a second mother to the younger ones—I wanted her to have a childhood of her own—but with so many children to care for, I leaned on the older ones. Especially Helen.

I knew she was going to make an amazing mother one day. Kindness just poured out of her.

"Smart," Billy said. "That must have distracted them a bit."

"They didn't know any better. They thought we were just having a party in the basement. But I did. It's happened four times before, in between baby number six, number eight, number nine, number eleven, and now after number thirteen. If she hadn't lost those babies, we'd be a family of eighteen kids. Eighteen," Bernadette said.

"I wonder if they were girls or boys," Veronica said.

"We wouldn't know. She and dad never talk about it," Bernadette said.

"Every time it happens, I can't help but worry even more for mom," said Helen.

"She's strong, don't forget that," Robbie said.

"I know she is, but each loss chips more and more of that strength away from her," Helen replied.

"And from us," Bernadette added.

"I know," Robbie said. "This time was, well, the hardest."

I'd never realized how much this weighed on them. They felt the loss of each child right along with me, and some of them were too young to even understand what was happening. Robert, Helen, and Bernadette clearly understood. When I looked back at the pictures, the years in between losing a child and having another were stark reminders.

"Jeez. That's like a whole baseball team," Billy said.

"Yeah, Billy. We know," Robert said.

"Bernadette kept saying it happened again, and I asked her what happened again," Veronica added.

"I told her there wouldn't be a christening this year," Bernadette explained.

No, we wouldn't be having another christening ever again because Dr. O had told me I *couldn't* have any more children.

"Well, at least you'll save some money on booze," Billy said.

"What the heck are you implying, Billy?" Robbie asked, raising his voice.

"Oh, come on, you know how the Irish like to drink at a party," Billy said, laughing to himself. "Or, you know, just a random Tuesday. "

"Oh, and the Polack's don't?" Robbie asked.

"Screw you! You piece of shit!"

"Piece of what? Get out! Get the hell out of our house!" Robbie yelled. I heard the kids pushing their chairs in and getting up as Billy ran out the front door. I hurried back to the stairs, careful not to be seen eavesdropping.

Bernadette had been right. Ted and I hadn't done a good job at addressing the years when we lost a child. I just never knew how to start. I was pregnant, and then I wasn't. They were smart kids and had been paying much closer attention than I gave them credit for. But this time, we needed to tell them there wouldn't be anymore. I thought some of them would be relieved, dare I say even happy, with the news, and that was going to be an even harder pill to swallow.

As much as I wanted to hug them all and tell them it was all okay, that I was okay, I didn't want them to know I had heard their whole conversation. And to be honest, I wasn't okay. I didn't want to lie to them and paint some rosy picture when the reality was I was grieving.

I tiptoed from the stairs to the living room when it sounded safe to make myself heard and walked over to where my piano used to be. In the years when I lost a baby, I would play Mahler's *Ich bin der Welt abhanden gekommen.* The translation of the lyrics in German mixed with the poignancy of the melody always made me cry, so when I had to hold in the pain and the tears, I would let my fingers do the crying for me. Without my piano, I couldn't even do that.

CHAPTER 29

THIRTEEN GIFTS

SAINT MICHAEL'S HOSPITAL, FALL—1960

The air felt sterile and empty as I laid in the hospital bed, and no matter how many blankets I put on, I just couldn't seem to get warm. There was a tray of stale, uneaten cafeteria food on the table next to my bed, a gray plastic pitcher of water, and some slimy-looking red Jell-O. Who could actually eat that stuff was beyond me. I had drawn the shades, but even the fluorescent lights felt blinding. I was groggy and then suddenly incredibly thirsty as I reached for the water and took a sip. I held my rosary beads and moved my fingers over them, praying for some good news as I waited for the doctor.

Dr. O'Connor came into my room as he looked over my chart, his expression looking graver than his usual pleasant demeanor.

"So, what's the prognosis Dr. O? When do you think I can try again?"

"Your body can't handle carrying another child," Dr. O'Connor said. "The risks are too great."

"What are you saying? What risks?" I asked.

"If you try to conceive again, you could die," Dr. O'Connor said. "But the good news is, you have options. The obvious one is birth control—"

"Doctor, I'm Catholic. We don't do birth control. You know that." Being so devoutly Catholic, I truly believed I needed my priest's permission to protect my body from having more children. I didn't actually need his permission, but I thought I did.

"I was getting to that. I called Father Donahue." As if they had timed it, Father Donahue walked into the room at that exact moment.

Father Donahue had baptized all the kids and was a big part of our lives. We were very involved in our local parish, St. Ann's, and went to mass every Sunday. He was there for so many family celebrations, baptisms, first communions, and confirmations over the years, and he was there for me again on that difficult day.

"Audrey, I'm going to give you a pardon to go on birth control," Father Donahue said. I couldn't believe he had just said that. While so many other families looked down on us for having so many children, Father Donahue was always supportive of how God kept blessing us with more. It just didn't seem right.

Yes, I might have been in my early forties at that point, but I was still strong and healthy. I was made to have babies.

"No. I can't."

"The Lord has given you thirteen gifts," Father Donahue said.

"I'm a mother. That's who I am. That's what I do."

"Audrey, you are a child of God, and he wants you to be able to care for the thirteen you have," Father Donahue said.

"I have spent the last twenty years carrying children. It's what I do, please. Please don't take that away from me too."

"In Jeremiah 29:11, he says, *'for I know the plans I have for you, plans to prosper you and not to harm you, plans to give you hope and a future.'* I will continue to pray for healing, for hope, and the bright future ahead for you and your children," Father Donahue said. I'd always loved that verse, and yet I thought about all I had lost already.

All those children, Bobby, my dreams, how could all that loss not be harming me? It sure felt like harm to me. Faith was believing in what we couldn't see and believing his plans were for our good. But gosh, it was a hard pill to swallow.

Trusting God for my present and my future was the ultimate question of faith. I just didn't know how much more loss I could take.

"Thank you, Father. It's just hard to think about the future right now."

"Of course. One day at a time," he said as there was a knock at the door. Dr. O stepped away to answer it.

"I invited someone to lift your spirits," Dr. O'Connor said. I saw a gorgeous bouquet of pink, purple and red flowers floating into the room, covering the guest's face. I knew from how elegant the arrangement was it was Rose. The flowers immediately brightened up the dull, dreary room, and I breathed in the sweet aroma. If only flowers could've made that situation better.

"I came as soon as I heard. Are you okay?" Rose asked. She came closer to the bed and took my hand in hers.

"She'll be all right if we can talk some sense into her." Dr. O'Connor turned to me and said, "We'll talk a little later when Ted gets off work." He started to leave the room and then said to Rose, "Don't stay too long. She needs to rest."

"God bless you, my child. I'll come by to see you again tomorrow," Father Donahue added.

I crossed myself and said, "Thank you, Father. And please, say a prayer for the five that are in heaven."

"Yes, Father, the six that are in heaven," Rose said.

"Of course. You'll both be in my prayers," Father Donahue said and then left Rose and I alone.

"Rose?" My mouth had dropped. Had I heard her right, she had lost a child? She avoided my eyes, rearranging the flowers nervously and not saying a word.

"Rose, come sit down. Talk to me," I urged her. She rearranged the flowers one more time and then reluctantly sat on my bed. I looked at her waiting for an explanation as she took my hand, looked me straight in the eye, and let out a long sigh.

"Oscar and I were newlyweds. I was too ashamed to tell you," Rose said.

"Why?" I asked.

"It was horrible. The pain was—" She couldn't finish, but I did for her as she started to cry.

"Unbearable." I knew all too well how unbearable the pain was.

"All this time, I thought you couldn't have children," I said.

"I was too afraid to ever go through the loss of a child again," she said.

"You went on birth control?" I asked, already wrestling with that decision myself.

"The pill didn't exist back then, and you know how the church viewed even condoms as a form of contraception. Abstinence was the only way."

"I don't think Ted would go for that, but Father Donahue gave me a pardon to go on birth control. I just don't know if I can," I said.

"Do it, Audrey. I couldn't bear losing you," Rose said.

"I gave up music to have children," I said.

"What does that have to do with anything?" Rose asked.

"If I can't have any more children, and I can't perform, then who am I?" I asked rhetorically but was really hoping Rose had an answer. I certainly didn't. I had no idea who I was if I wasn't having more children or wasn't performing. What was my purpose now? I could hear the director's voice ringing in my ear, telling me to go back to being a housewife. Just remembering those words left a bitter taste in my mouth.

"Audrey," Rose said, squeezing my hand ever so gently. I couldn't hold the tears in anymore, and with Rose's kindness, they started pouring out. "You're more than a performer and mother. What did Father Donahue just say? You're a child of God." Her words were comforting but made me cry even more.

Rose climbed into the bed and held me. She was the closest thing I had to a sister and a mother, having lost my mom years ago, and she started to stroke my hair gently, just like I did with my girls when they were upset or trying to fall asleep.

"My mom used to always say God has a plan. Even in this," Rose said. I started to catch my breath, and Rose handed me a tissue to wipe my tears and blow my nose. I took another sip of water and was starting to collect myself when I remembered what Rose had said about her and Oscar.

"Wait a minute. If you didn't go on birth control, and you *can* have children—"

"I told Oscar we could never have sex again," Rose said.

"What?" She hadn't had sex with her husband in twenty-plus years? How on earth had that worked? I could not believe she never told me any of this and had been carrying this burden all by herself. She must have been so lonely. I wrapped myself up in the chaos of raising thirteen kids. I didn't even notice what was happening with my best friend. I felt horrible.

"No more heartache, no more loss. I needed to be in control," Rose said. "Yet in that control…"

"You lost something," I finished.

"I robbed us of the chance to be parents," Rose said.

"Oh, Rose."

"I pushed him into the arms of other women," Rose continued.

"No, Rose. Oscar could never—"

"He has. I pushed him, us, too far. I don't know how we can come back from this," Rose whispered.

"It's not too late. You can start over with Oscar," I said.

"How?" she asked.

"Marriage is complicated, but I truly believe at the core, you both still love each other," I said. It was the understatement of the century. I knew how much they loved each other. I had watched them and been in their company for decades. There was so much love there.

"We do. Well, I know I do," Rose said.

"I want to be clear about something, though. There's no excusing he's been with other women, if that's the truth. He made that choice. You didn't push him."

"I know. We both made our choices," Rose said.

"Do you think you can forgive him? Or do you even want to?" I asked.

"I'm hurt, of course, and angry, but I've dealt with my reality for years and have come to accept our situation as normal. So, I think I can forgive him. We are both flawed, and I think there is power in forgiveness."

"Then you have to try," I said. She hugged me and kissed me on the cheek, climbed out of my bed, and turned to me on her way out.

"Are you going to be okay?" she asked.

"I think so. Are you?"

"Yes. I think so too." She left with determination. I felt like a weight lifted off my shoulders, and I had a feeling it lifted from Rose's too.

Ted walked in shortly after Rose had left and looked completely distraught and scared. He sat on my bed and kissed me on my forehead.

"Oh Ted, I'm so glad you are here," I said.

"I should've been home when this happened," he said.

"You were at work," I said.

"I should have been with you."

"We have thirteen children. You needed to work," I said.

He put his head in his hands, and I could see he was beating himself up over it, but really, what could he have done? Nothing other than take me to the hospital, and we were lucky Dr. O'Connor had been home.

"The doctor wants me to go on the pill."

"If the doctor said that's what's best, I think we should listen to him," Ted said.

"Would you really be okay with us not having any more children? Would you still look at me the same way?" I asked.

"Audrey, you seem to forget I fell in love with you long before you were the mother of my children. I love you for who you are, not for how many children you have given me." He kissed me, and it reminded me again what an amazing man I married.

"Oh, Ted. I want to be around to take care of the thirteen we have, but I'm scared."

"I'm more scared of losing you. Please listen to the doctor, if not for the kids and me, then for yourself. You have so much more life to live."

"That I do," I said.

CHAPTER 30

ALONG THE WAY

ROSE: ROSE AND OSCAR'S APARTMENT, WINTER—1960

"The door will be open tonight… if you'd like to *stay*," I said into the mirror after brushing my hair and spraying my temples and wrists with perfume. I breathed in the lily of the valley floral scent and lowered my blush pink satin robe, showing off my shoulders.

"The door will be *open* tonight if you'd like to stay." I practiced saying the words again. No, that didn't seem right either.

I flipped my head forward and shook my hair out to be messy and loose around my shoulders. I slowly started to untie my robe and looked right into the mirror.

"The door will be open tonight *if* you'd like to stay," I said again with a sultry whisper. I didn't even recognize that voice. I couldn't remember how to flirt with my husband. I was so out of practice. What would Audrey have done? She'd probably just come right out and say it, but I couldn't be that bold. I looked back at my reflection, thinking of what I needed, lipstick, of course! I took out some red lipstick and started to apply it when I heard the front door to the apartment open. I ran into the living room, determined he would not leave tonight. I just had to convince him.

"Oscar? Where are you going?" I asked.

"I—I have a late meeting at the theater," he said.

"Oscar, please don't go tonight."

"I'm sorry, but I have someone waiting for me. I have to go," he said impatiently, opening the door to leave.

"*I'm* someone who's waiting for you."

"Rose, I didn't—"

"I'm waiting for you, and I'm right here," I said, and the words just started pouring out of me.

Along the Way

ROSE
I remember the night we met
sewing costumes at the theater
In walked this dashing man

OSCAR
Your face was as delicate as lace

ROSE
So much elegance in the palm of your hand

ROSE/OSCAR
I was so distracted from watching you

ROSE
I pricked my finger with the needle

OSCAR
I spilled my coffee on the table

ROSE
You kissed the tip to stop the bleeding

OSCAR
You brushed my hand while you were cleaning

OSCAR/ROSE
And I knew it was you I was needing
But along the way, I pushed you away
I was so scared

ROSE
To lose a child again

OSCAR
I've cheated for years
And I paid with your tears

ROSE/OSCAR
We can't get those years back
But I'm ready to try along the way

ROSE/OSCAR
Can we can start again?
Can we make anew?
Can we love again?
Can I forgive you?

ROSE

I'm so sorry Oscar.

OSCAR

No, I'm the one who is sorry, Rose.

ROSE/OSCAR

We can start again
We can make a new
We can love again
I forgive you
Along the way
Along the way
We'll fall in love again
Along the way

Oscar embraced me, and it felt so good to be in his arms again. I had forgotten what it felt like, human touch and the comfort of him. We sat down on the couch, he poured me a glass of wine, and I couldn't help but notice how handsome he looked, as the moonlight seeped in through the terrace window. We each took a sip, and I could feel all the tension and pressure we both had been holding in for years just slowly start to breathe air back into the room.

We had a long way to go, and I didn't think our marriage challenges had all been washed away in one night, but I was hopeful. The communication lines were open again, and that was a huge step forward.

"I'm glad you stopped me from leaving tonight," he admitted.

"I'm glad you stayed long enough to listen."

"It's nice to see you fighting for us. I wasn't sure what you wanted anymore."

"I know. I wasn't sure what you wanted either. Losing Grace changed me in ways I never imagined."

"You named her Grace? You never told me that."

"I know. I never told anyone her name."

"I lost a child too, Rose." His eyes mirrored the pain I had been carrying on my own for years.

"I'm sorry I didn't let you in," I said and took his hand in mine.

"I'm sorry I didn't have the words to comfort you," he said, putting his arm around me as I laid my head on his shoulder.

"I know it's too late for us to have our own children, and for that, I will never forgive myself, but Audrey and Ted do seem to have quite a few we could spend more time with as Aunt Rose and Uncle Oscar. I was thinking, wouldn't it be lovely to keep passing our love of the theater onto them? "I asked.

"Aunt Rose and Uncle Oscar—I've always liked the sound of that. If you think about it, it's like having all the best parts of being parents, but we get to give them back at the end of the night," Oscar said with a laugh.

"Yes! We get to spoil them and not discipline them. I did love taking them to their first Broadway show. Audrey was so thrilled, and the awe on the kids' faces as the curtain opened and the orchestra played the overture," I said.

"They practically jumped out of their seats," Oscar said.

"And Jane snuggled right up into my lap," I remembered fondly.

Patrick kept whispering, "Can they see us, Uncle Oscar?"

"We really are lucky, aren't we?" I asked.

"We are, and I think it's time to take them to another show. Maybe a comedy this time?" he suggested.

"Oh, Oscar, that would be so fun!" I exclaimed.

"It's settled then," Oscar said. "I'll make the arrangements first thing in the morning."

"Thank you, Oscar. Your generosity never ceases to amaze me. Now I think there are a few *other* arrangements that need tending to…" I said with more confidence than I felt. Nervously I started to untie my silk robe and dropped my voice like I had practiced in the mirror earlier that night. "The door will be open tonight if you'd like to stay." I felt like a silly schoolgirl trying to play the role of a sexy movie star, but I did it anyway. Oscar's eyes lit up in surprise, and I could see after all these years, he still desired me.

"I'd like that very much," he said. I took his hand and squeezed it gently, smiling coyly back at him.

ROSE: JANE'S HOUSE, THANKSGIVING—1992

"I'm so glad you and Uncle Oscar found your way back to each other," Amelia says, wiping a tear from her eye.

"I am too," I say as I glance up at the window and can't believe it's dark already. Audrey and I had been talking to Amelia all day and well into the night. Most of the family had already gone home by now. Someone had cleared the dinner dishes, and all that was left were a few slices of pie and coffee cups on the table.

"Thank you for sharing your stories with me. I don't think I could've handled the loss, the heartbreak, and the lack of agency that was just your reality back then," Amelia says.

"Of course, you could've! You're a girl…" I start.

"Your Irish, you can do anything!" Amelia and Audrey both chime in, and we all laugh.

"Exactly, and it's not our reality anymore, is it Rose?" Audrey says.

"No, and we are not going to waste time trying to control everything…" I reply.

"*Or* blending in… I hope you can learn from our past. You have so much ahead of you," Audrey says.

"I have, and I've got some big shoes to fill," Amelia says, squeezing both mine and Audrey's hands. "So, what's next for both of you?" Amelia asks.

I look at Audrey with a big grin, and we both say: "Anything we want!"

ACT 3

CHAPTER 31

MATERNAL INSTINCTS

ROSE: NEW YORK CITY, WINTER—1993

After Oscar died, I needed someone to take care of. It was too quiet in the apartment. The piano sat there lonely, and I was lonely too. I needed to feel useful again, and without the constant after-parties and social events to host, the overwhelming quiet and constant free time almost killed me. With Audrey's encouragement, I followed up at Mount Sinai Hospital. Despite my insecurities of not having a lifetime of mothering experience, they were happy to have me as a volunteer in the nursery.

I walk from Central Park West down twenty blocks three days a week. The fresh air and exercise are good for me both physically and mentally. Walking in New York with a purpose, I blend right in. All New Yorkers walk as if on their way to the most important meeting of their life, so I walk briskly and smile to myself, knowing I have an important meeting three times a week with the next generation of New Yorkers.

I make my way up the elevator at the hospital to the twenty-seventh floor and check in at the front desk, smiling at the nurses and assistants who have become part of my new work family. The receptionist hands me a chart with an updated list of all the current babies in the nursery and the mothers they expect to give birth today. The nurses on the delivery floor are some of the hardest-working women I've ever met. Their hands are dry from the constant washing, their lips chapped from hours in cold operating rooms, and their eyes are bloodshot from working twenty-four-hour shifts. Yet, they still greet their patients with warm smiles, displaying empathy and strength in everything they do.

I have such a small part to play, but I'm thankful to be able to provide the newborns with love and attention while their mothers are recovering from delivery, trying to sleep and heal. I walk into the nursery, mentally checking the rows of clear bassinets and the pink and blue precious beanie hats on the newborn's heads, some of them sleeping swaddled just so and a few fussing and ready to be held.

Charlie was born just three hours ago, according to his bassinet label, and I cross-check with my chart. His cries meowed like a baby kitten. Reaching into the bassinet, I pick him up and gently rock him.

"Shhh, there, there, little Charlie, it's going to be okay," I whisper. His cry softening when the door opens to a surprise visitor.

"Who let you in here?" I ask.

"The nurse did. I was in the neighborhood and thought I'd pop in for a visit," Audrey says.

"Well, this is a surprise," I say.

"I brought you a tea and some scones," Audrey says as she places them down on a table.

"That's very thoughtful of you."

"And who are we holding today?" Audrey asks.

"This is Charlie."

"What a perfect prince! Charles is such a strong name," Audrey says.

"On no, this is just Charlie, not Charles," I say.

"Well, it seems they've given the prince only half a name, but it is wonderful to see you with all these little ones!"

"I do love their itty-bitty toes and sighs they make... and that baby smell!" I say, gently squeezing Charlie's toes.

Audrey leans in and sniffs the top of Charlie's head with a sigh. "New baby smell is intoxicating," Audrey says.

"No wonder you had one every year!" I say as we both laugh.

"Now you know my secret."

Another baby wails, and I gently hand Charlie over to Audrey, who instinctively puts him in the nook of her arm and sways back and forth, as I'm sure she's done countless times with her children. She seems to do so effortlessly. I'm curious if it will ever come as naturally to me. Can you have maternal instincts if you are not a mother?

"I know that cry. It's the 'I'm hungry cry,'" Audrey says. I nod in agreement and walk to the counter to quickly make a bottle.

"It's funny how infants only have one way to communicate at this stage, barely in the world for twenty-four hours, and yet I'm learning how to differentiate the cries. The 'I'm wet' cry versus the 'I'm hungry' cry and the 'I want my mom cry.'"

"You are a natural! I didn't know the difference in the early days. All the cries sounded the same to me. I'd just look at this creature screaming back at me, and I'd want to ask them, what's wrong? Can you just tell me, and then I can make that noise stop so I can go back to sleep?" says Audrey.

"Ha! I can't even imagine. I get to give these screaming creatures back to their moms and comfortably go back home to sleep. But from what I'm observing, newborns clearly can communicate their wants; change me, feed me, love me. You just have to pay attention and listen."

"Exactly, and I'm hoping you'll listen to me next. I promise I won't cry, but I've come with a proposition."

"I was wondering to what I owed this impromptu visit. All right, I'm listening." I walk up to another bassinet and pick up the 'I'm hungry' crier and feed her a bottle.

"I just got a call from Veronica, and Amelia is in Dublin this semester. I just thought, well, we've never been, and I just know there are some amazing pianos I've yet to find between St. Patrick's Cathedral and Trinity College. Ooh, we could even go to Cork and Kildare, where our family is from!"

"Ireland! Wow, well, that would be quite a trip. But I don't know Audrey. I haven't traveled like that since Oscar died. Besides, these little darlings need me here."

"Oh Rose, we've never gone on an international girl's trip before! Think of how liberating it would be for us. No husbands, no children, just imagine having a little adventure, just for us."

I burp the princess I just fed, patting her on the back and bouncing up and down a bit.

"An adventure, huh?" I'm still not convinced.

"Yes! Please, say yes. Oh, we will have so much fun!"

"You know, I don't even think I have an updated passport."

"Oh, don't be silly. I'm sure we can pay extra to get you one in the next few weeks. We can go after your shift is over."

I know it seems like a great idea, but they really depend on me here. I'm having so much fun taking care of these sweet things. A trip right now, let alone an international one, just feels extravagant. I'm honestly surprised Audrey suggested this. I wonder what's really going on with her. She wouldn't have come all the way here to ask me in person if she didn't *really* need me or need this trip. It is nice to feel needed, and who am I to judge what my friend needs right now. I seem to have just talked myself out of it and into it.

"You are persistent… Do you think we could see a show while we are there? I have always wondered what theater is like outside of New York and The West End." The idea of theater in Ireland does pique my fancy.

"Of course! Pianos and shows and family heritage!"

"And shopping with my great-niece?"

"Yes, we will spoil her rotten."

Theater, family heritage, and getting to spend quality girl time with Amelia seals the deal for me. I love taking her to shows and dinner and finding the perfect outfit. Living vicariously through her youth makes me feel young again. She has a unique taste in fashion and is such a theater kid. It breaks my heart Oscar didn't get to get to know her as well as I have.

"It's settled then. We are going to Ireland!" I say. Audrey echoes with a squeal of delight.

"Shh! You'll wake the babies!"

"Sorry, I'm just so excited!"

"Me too! I can call Oscar's old travel agent and get everything arranged for us."

"You are an angel, Rose. Thank you! I'll leave you to the babies, and I'm off to meet Dr. O for lunch!"

Audrey leaves in a whirlwind, and I'm left here with diapers to change and bottles to clean, smiling at how our lives have suddenly or not so suddenly flip-flopped. I'm happy for her. She deserves to be taking care of no one except herself and being woo'd and wined by an eligible doctor.

But a trip without men, without children, just us girls, now that is special. I sing a little lullaby to baby Charlie as my daydreams wander off into what we'll see and experience in Ireland.

It's Never too Late

ROSE
It's never too late
to grab ahold of your dreams
it's never too late
to reach for the stars
It's never too late
It's never too late to try

As I rock and sing him to sleep, Charlie closes his eyes and nestles into my shoulder. I gently lay him back into his bassinet on his stomach, and he scrunches his arms and feet together, sticking his little tush up in the air. I can't help but smile, thinking he looks like a baby frog. He looks so content.

I didn't get to rock my own baby to sleep, but maybe it's time to let that dream go and look ahead to the life I have in front of me and not the one I left behind me.

CHAPTER 32

ANGELS, ANCESTORS, AND PIANOS

AUDREY: DUBLIN IRELAND, SPRING—1993

Family heritage has always intrigued me. How do people identify with a nationality and culture even if they've never physically been to that country of origin? I've always related strongly to my Irish heritage and having the opportunity to travel to where my ancestors are from at this stage in my life is thrilling.

My parents instilled values of faith, family, hard work, loyalty, and to always speak your mind. Do those values make me "Irish" or Irish American? Or am I Irish purely from the history of our family's origin? Is it in my blood, or is it passed down in the values that my parents, and their parents before them, passed down? I'd like to think I've passed down those same values to my children and grandchildren.

Going to mass on Sunday, raising your children with faith, volunteering your time and talents in the church community and the broader local community are just a few. Along with driving for excellence in anything you do and believing that hard work and education are the two things that no one can take from you, regardless of where you started. There's always room for one more at the dinner table, and celebrating the holidays with laughter, music, and family is better than any gift you could ever buy in a store.

I see my children living their lives all very differently but also embracing so many of these values and traditions in their own families. Seeing Amelia follow her dreams, studying musical theater, and experiencing things I never had the opportunity to in my youth, makes me incredibly proud. As Rose and I roll our suitcases across the gray cobblestone street, Amelia comes running through the hotel's doors full of youthful energy.

"Grandma, Aunt Rose, you made it! I'm so excited to see you both!"

"You know Rose and I have always wanted to come to Ireland," I say, giving her a big hug.

"I'm sure you both are tired from the trip here. I'll go get the hotel staff to bring your bags upstairs, and we can sit and have some tea before destination one on our itinerary."

"Thank you, dear. Tea sounds perfect," Rose says.

"Itinerary, huh? You've got everything planned, do you?" I ask with a smile.

"Obviously. You can't accomplish your goals without a plan, and what's that thing you always tell me, 'We make a goal and get out of our way?'"

"She really is a McKenna, isn't she?" Rose asks.

"She sure is."

"I want to make sure you both have the Best time ever!" Amelia says, notably earnest to ensure our trip lives up to the years of expectation. As the bellhop takes our bags, she leads us to a dining room. One of the waiters sits us down, and we order our drinks.

"I was wondering if you could tell me a little bit about our family history?" Amelia asks as I take a sip of my tea.

"Of course! It's only fitting we talk about our family history while in Ireland."

"Awesome, because I have a paper I'm working on for one of my English classes titled *My Immigrant Saga*. It's super fun. We are reading all these books about different ethnic cultures and the history of how they immigrated to New York City, the different neighborhoods they lived in, and the trades they practiced."

"Wow. That does sound interesting. So, what would you like to know?"

"Well, for starters, can you tell me about how our family ended up in New York?"

I tell Amelia everything I know about our history, from the McGrath's in New York City to the Kelly's in Boston. I tell her how her great-great-grandfathers each made their way to America in the 1800s from Friars Grange, in the county of Tipperary. I tell her about the dances they went to, the women they met, and how they each met her great-great-grandmothers. I share how we came from big families, where having ten children was common.

But what she is most interested in is the music. A lot of the music traditions stemmed from our faith and singing hymns and songs in church. But it was most prevalent on the Kelly side of the family, my mother's side. My grandmother loved to sing, but my mother didn't get the music gene. Maybe that's why she never encouraged it. My talent reminded her she was different and often left out when the Kelly's would gather and sing together. How ironic to think my mother might have felt that way when she made me feel the same; different and left out.

I tell her about a scandal that a distant cousin of ours, Croddy Kelly, was a coachman, and he married a daughter of the house. He fell in love with her because she used to sing and play the piano every afternoon, and he would wait by the door to listen to her play. The opposing side tragically killed him at Antietam during the Civil War, and her family disowned her for marrying beneath her.

"Wow, and all of that started from a woman singing and playing the piano," Amelia says.

"The power of music is part of our family heritage," I say.

"Speaking of heritage. I have a few surprises for us today. Are you ready for destination one?"

"Yes!" Rose and I both say in unison.

"Great, come with me."

We follow Amelia down the street from the hotel and sit down in a town square. I'm taking in everything around me and trying to savor each piece of the puzzle fitting together. The bustle of the street reminds me of New York. It's just another typical spring day for the Dubliners drinking their coffee, commuters waiting in line at the bus stop on the corner, and children, backpacks in tow, holding onto their parent's hands on their way to school. For a country so well known for its gorgeous green landscapes, this morning, the colors of the city around me are cool grays and blues.

Rose and I peer over a small bridge out to the River Liffey, flanked with trees and restaurants primed for a river view. The crystal blue sky has the perfect amount of flat white clouds that look even lighter against the industrial feel of the dark greenish-black water, reminding me of a cleaner Hudson River. I sing to myself as I lean across the bridge, daydreaming.

The World Outside

AUDREY
There's a world outside
That I've never seen
There's A world outside
And places in between
There's adventure in the air
as the wind blows through my hair
There's a world outside
I just can't wait to see

In the center of the square is a monument of sorts, carved out of gray stone, and on opposite sides of the monument are two majestic angels sculpted out of metal. Their wings look both heavy and light with sharp pointed edges. Their presence grounds me in both the peace of my faith and knowing my family of angels are watching out for me everywhere.

Amelia escorts Rose and I to folding chairs set up in rows in front of the monument, and as we are taking our seats, a young girl and boy, around eight or nine, head to the center in traditional Irish dancing costumes. The girl's blond hair piled on top of her head has perfect curls placed and teased just so, and shiny sequins cover her dress mixed with white, red, green, and black stitching. The boy, slightly older and taller, has curly, chestnut brown hair, which is striking against his pale skin and deep blue eyes.

I can't help but see a memory of Bobby and I at that age. The children start clogging away, and Rose and I are happily clapping along to the music. Rose was watching intently and focused on something, but what that is, I don't know.

My eyes wander from Rose and the children to a rustic upright piano and the adorable little old man playing with gusto. His salt and pepper hair reminds me of Dr. O and our first date in Little Italy. I remember what it felt like to dance with him for the first time. I hope he's keeping busy and not worrying about me. I mean, oh, I don't know. I kind of do want him to be worrying or at least thinking of me.

My fingers silently move in the air, longingly wanting to play just like they did that night in New York. As the music seems to get louder, the children are joined by adult dancers as they make a line. The dancers encourage the audience to join them, and the energy of music and dancing fills the town square.

"Why don't you try it, Grandma!" Amelia says.

"Oh no, I couldn't."

"Audrey, we are girls, we are Irish and in Ireland! We can do anything!" Rose cheers, grabbing mine and Amelia's hands and pulling us up onto the dance floor. We clumsily attempt to follow the dancers, laughing together with each step. After a few minutes, Rose and I both collapse onto our chairs, worn out from dancing. Amelia is still dancing along, her smile wide and eyes bright with youthful energy and determination.

"Look at those children! I wonder how old they were when they first started dancing?" Rose asks.

"Probably as soon as they could walk," I reply and dab the sweat from my brow with a napkin.

"Hmm. You know when you asked me what I wanted to do next?" Rose asks.

"Sure, you already started volunteering in the nursery," I say.

"Right, but... listen for a minute. I'm thinking, what if I was a talent agent, like Oscar?"

"Huh. Well, that would be interesting *and* exciting."

"I think so too, but for *children*, not adults," Rose clarifies.

"Well, you certainly have an eye for talent."

"And I do know the New York theater scene." The volume and energy in Rose's voice increase along with her confidence, and I can see all the wheels turning in her head.

"Then go for it, Rose," I say. As soon as she said children, and New York theater, her entire face lit up like someone just plugged in the lights on a Christmas tree. She's been scouting for years, right beside Oscar. Why shouldn't she have something just for her? I'm excited for her. "I'm rooting for you!"

Amelia comes back to our chairs, balancing three pints of Guinness.

"Who's thirsty? You have to have a Guinness. It's like a milkshake!" says Amelia.

"It's barely ten o'clock in the morning! What are you doing having a beer?" Rose asks.

"Aunt Rose, please. The drinking age is eighteen, and consider this an early brunch," she says like she's done this before.

"Oh Rose, come on, let's live a little!" I say.

"Exactly, that's what you are here for! To experience Ireland," Amelia says.

"Oh, all right," Rose relents with a smile.

"To the Murphy's and the McKenna's!" I cheer, holding up my Guinness.

"And the Kelly's!" Rose adds as we clank our pints and all take a big gulp. The frothy beer is thick as I get a mixed taste of coffee, chocolate, and beer. I can understand why Amelia called it a milkshake. This could fill you up very quickly and tastes completely different from beer at home.

While I want to spend time having new experiences here, the rustic piano catches my eye again, and it reminds me of my bigger mission here. Amelia might have our itinerary all mapped out, but I have plans of my own as well.

"Now, Amelia, I hope the rest of the afternoon is free because there is a piano I'm looking for."

"What kind of piano?" Amelia asks as she takes another sip of her beer.

"Well, I was reading that there is a Dublin made upright by John Robert Woffington dating back to the 1800s."

"Wow. That is extremely specific."

"I know. I'm on the hunt for unique pianos."

"Well, let's go find you that piano! Hmm, pianos, pianos… maybe the music school at Trinity College has one?"

"It's worth a shot!" I say.

On our way to Trinity, we stop at Murdock's, a famous fish and chips place. The fried cod and chips are wrapped in brown paper and battered ever so lightly they just melt in your mouth with the perfect amount of crunch and salt. The owner of Murdock's, Rory Murdock, talks our ears off as he proudly shares the history of this little stand and how tourists travel from all over the world to come to get a taste. As he goes on about his family, it's so clear that our 'gift of gab' is not just an Irish American trait but one that runs deep in our Irish culture.

A gentle breeze blows pink flower petals around our feet, and we all agree that while we could sit here on this bench all day, it's time to look for that piano. Amelia leads the way as we leisurely walk toward the college. On our way, we pass pub after pub, each with a different yet familiar Irish moniker, O'Hara's, Buckley's, Mulligan's, M.J, O'Neil's. It makes me smile thinking of all the Irish families I grew up with and knowing where they came from.

"Look Rose, O'Hara's! Do you remember that O'Hara boy that used to play with Bobby?"

"The one with the green eyes and the killer smile?"

"Good memory," I say.

"Yes, he was a dreamboat," she says, and we both wink at each other, and Amelia chuckles at us.

After making our way through several streets of pubs, we arrive at Trinity College. The campus is buzzing with both the energy of students and tourists like us visiting this historic landmark. The slate gray stone buildings with rows and rows of windows look more like old estate mansions than college buildings, with bicycles in all pastel colors parked out front along the green grass. We wander into a hushed library filled with little nooks and crannies of wired spiral staircases and the highest arched ceilings I've ever seen. The deep mahogany wood and rows and rows of books filled with history feel just as sacred as walking through the pews of St. Patrick's cathedral.

Amelia leads us through the library and out to the music school. I feel like a peeping tom popping my head into practice rooms, scanning for pianos once we arrive. I love hearing the range of music coming from the rooms, everything from opera to jazz, classical to rock. We stop at Professor Byrne's office, and Amelia knocks on the door.

"Come in." Professor Byrne looks up from a pile of papers we interrupted him from reviewing.

"Hi, Professor Byrne? I'm Amelia! I'm in the Musical Theater Program from Syracuse this semester."

"Hi Amelia, how can I help you?" he asks, moving his tiny reading glasses down a bit farther onto his nose.

"Well, this is my Grandma Audrey and Great Aunt Rose, and we were wondering if there was—what's it called again, Grandma?"

"A Woffington piano, dear."

"Right, we were wondering if there was a Woffington piano hiding on campus somewhere?"

"What is your interest in a Woffington piano?" Professor Byrne asks.

"It's a long story, but I've been on sort of a piano treasure hunt this year looking for antique and rare pianos, and this one with its Irish history just sounded fascinating," I say.

"I see. What an interesting adventure. Unfortunately, I'm not aware of any such piano on campus, but I can give you some names of piano stores in the area if you'd like."

"Oh, that would be wonderful! Thank you!" I say.

"Thanks, Professor!" Amelia echoes. We make our way out of the music school and back to the hotel, tired from a very full first day of adventure.

Amelia filled our days to the brim with museums, Irish culture, a tour of the Guinness factory, and we even caught a show one night which made Rose so happy. She had her chance of spoiling Amelia with some shopping as well. In between Amelia's jam-packed itinerary, we searched for the Woffington piano.

The hunt for the piano was exhilarating as it had forced Rose, Amelia, and I to explore all over the city, even in places that were not on Amelia's itinerary. We scoured over ten different antique shops across Dublin and even took a day trip out of the city to a small suburb of Leixlip one day. I loved seeing the rolling hills of greenery, and the locals were so friendly and welcoming. It was a fun little excursion even though we didn't find the Woffington there.

We finally found it in an antique piano store that was ready to ship it to London for auction. I was afraid to really play it. It was so delicate. The ivory keys were yellowed, and several of them chipped or missing altogether. As satisfying as it was to find the Woffington piano, it *wasn't* the piano. The one that would make this hunt complete and quench my thirst. I didn't know exactly what I was searching for, but I had a hunch I'd know it when I saw it.

As I lay my head down on the pillow in my hotel room at the end of the week, I'm already dreaming of angels, pianos, and my ancestors. I was exhausted from this trip and in a deep sleep when the phone startled me out of bed. Instinctively I reach out and pick it up.

"Hello?" I ask, my voice thick with sleep.

"Audrey! I'm sorry, did I wake you?" Dr. O's voice fills my ear from the other end of the phone.

"Oh, Dr. O! Not at all. I was just getting up. How are you?"

"Oh, all is good back in the states. I just wanted to check on you."

"What time is it there? I'm all disoriented with the time changes," I question.

"It's four in the afternoon. When is your flight home?" he asks.

"Rose and I get in next Saturday."

"Got it. Are you two having a good time? How's Amelia?"

"Yes, we are having a wonderful time. Amelia is quite the little tour guide."

"That's great. I'm so happy to hear that. I'm sure Amelia is loving living abroad."

"She is, and Rose and I *love* experiencing it with her."

"Of course. I know you are having a family adventure right now, but have you thought any more about..."

"I just—I just need a little more time."

"Audrey, it's been…"

"I know. I'm sorry. Goodnight."

He wants an answer, but I don't have time to think about proposals right now, as there are more adventures ahead of me and pianos to find.

CHAPTER 33

OPENING DOORS

ROSE: MORTY MAGORSKY'S OFFICE, NEW YORK CITY—1993

I'm not a wife going to visit her husband at work this morning. I'm a businesswoman on a mission to create the job I want, that I know I can do. My hot-pink power suit is making me stand up straighter as I walk through the subway doors crowded with professionals commuting downtown to their jobs. I smile at the other women in the subway car and realize that there are so many more women dressed for work than when I was a young woman—my how things have changed.

I emerge from the subway on forty-second and eighth avenue, sliding my sunglasses on to shield my eyes from the sun. I smile at the bright lights and bustle of times square and marvel at the transformation of this city in the sixty-plus years I've lived here. Oscar would be amazed at how the theater world has exploded with new sounds, styles, and the commercialism of Broadway. He always loved the classics, call him a purist that way, but talent is talent, and a good idea is a good idea. He taught me that.

I haven't been to Oscar's office building in years, but I'm channeling his business savvy this morning and wonder what he would think about this idea as I get into the elevator and push ten. Other than sewing in the costume shop, I've never had a paying job after Oscar, and I got married. I loved my volunteer time at the hospital, but this is different. There is a lot I don't know about the business, but there is so much more I do know. Pay attention to the nuances and pay attention to what audiences are responding to. Each generation finds themselves pulled toward something different, so what is this generation responding to?

Morty Magorsky was Oscar's boss for over twenty years. He took him under his wing, showed him the ropes, and treated him like a son. In those early years of working for Morty, I would come to visit Oscar, bring him a picnic lunch, and we would walk to Bryant Park and sit in the grass and talk. I miss those days. The more successful Oscar became, the less time he had for lunches with anyone other than potential clients, talent, or investors.

I imagine having my name on an office door and telling people *I'm* too busy for lunch. Unless it's Audrey, I'll always have time for lunch with her.

I think of Audrey's determination, resilience, and her travels around the world, and it inspires my courage. I can do this. I knock on the door, and there's Morty in all his glory. His bald head has a sheen of sweat on the top like a glazed doughnut, and I can see a coffee stain on his shirt, and one button is missing where his gut is sticking out. Suddenly I'm no longer nervous. He's just an old man from Brooklyn.

"Morty!" I say and kiss him on both cheeks, and he kisses me back.

"Sweetheart, you look better than ever! Come in, come in, take a seat," he says.

I look a lot better than you do, I think, giggling to myself. "Oh, you are too kind. I come bearing gifts." He starts to sit in his swivel chair behind his desk, and I can hear the weight of him settle with a thump. I hand him the bottle of Irish whisky I brought back from the trip, and his eyes light up.

"Ooh, now this really is my lucky day!" he says.

"I was in Dublin recently, and I remembered how much you liked your whisky," I reply.

"That I do. So, doll face, what can I do you for?" he asks. He opens the bottle of whisky, his chubby fingers fumbling with the cap. He brings the bottle to his nose and takes a whiff, reaches for two glasses next to his desk, and pours one for each of us. It's real early for whisky, but I just smile and accept the glass when he slides it toward me.

"Well, when I was in Dublin, I saw these two incredibly talented Irish dancers. They couldn't have been more than ten years old," I say.

"Is that right?" He takes a sip of the whisky while I leave mine.

"Yes, and it just got me thinking, with Oscar gone and all those nights I spent at the theater scouting talent with him…"

"Yeah…" He takes another sip of whisky and examines the bottle. He's not even listening to a word I'm saying. I should've waited to give him the whisky *after* I got his attention.

"I would like to pick up where he left off. But let me just scout for kids, not adults."

"For kids, huh?" he asks.

"Yes, just think, it could be a whole new division you haven't even tapped into yet!" I say.

"Now, I think it's really sweet you want to work with kids, but you have zero experience. Oscar did this for over thirty years!"

"Who do you think accompanied him to the theater, gave him suggestions, and opened his eyes to shows he never would've gone to? And… and… who entertained all his cronies and connections from every theater in this town?"

"Honey, that was your *job*—as his wife," he says.

"Oh my God, Morty, you can't talk to women like that! It's not the 1940s anymore. It's the 90s, for goodness' sake!" I point out.

"What? What'd I say?" he asks. He doesn't have a clue. I almost feel bad for him, but if Morty doesn't get it, someone who is practically family, how is anyone else going to get it and take a chance on me? I never even had a shot. I'm going to have to make this dream happen for myself.

"Aaah! You still don't get it! And for the record, I'm not his wife anymore, and I'd like a real job, one that's gonna make a difference for talented kids."

"I'm sorry, sweetheart, this old dog ain't ready to learn some new tricks."

"Do you even remember my name? Because it's not sweetheart."

"Oh, relax, of course, I do, but you're on your own. Thanks for the whisky. It was very thoughtful of you," he says as he throws the rest of the whisky back in one big gulp.

"Fine! If you don't hire me, I'll just start my own agency!" I get up and furiously walk toward the door.

"Yeah, okay. Good luck with that, honey," Morty says.

"My name's Rose!" And with that, I slam the door behind me, ready for the next door I'll open myself.

CHAPTER 34

PIANOS AND FISH

AUDREY: AUDREY'S HOUSE, SUMMER—1993

I think I've always felt like I was ten steps behind the men in my life.

When I was young, I was trying to catch up with Bobby and the gang. I resented I couldn't do everything the boys could do or have the freedom to make some of the choices they made. I hit a lot of brick walls. Walls society had put up or perceived walls I created myself.

When Rose told me the story about how Morty treated her and her idea to be an agent, it mortified me. I was mortified by Morty. How could he just dismiss her like that? I bet he was sorry now. She had started her own agency without anyone's help, and it was now a major success. She knocked down the wall standing in front of her, and she was her own boss now.

I have the chance to knock down some walls just like her.

Bobby and I used to sing to each other, "Nothing can stop the McKenna's; we make a goal, get out of our way." I set the goal to travel the world for unique pianos, and

I'm doing it. It's been nonstop traveling for over a year, and I've never been so excited to wake up every morning. I feel like I'm doing something just for me, for once in my life. But that also comes with a price to pay. I've neglected Dr. O.

When you get a taste of being an independent woman, well, it's hard to want to go backward. I've loved traveling with Dr. O and the adventures we've had together, but I've also learned I do really, really love traveling by myself.

I'm enjoying a nice cup of tea before bed and flipping through a book about the music history of Nashville. I can hear the music through the black and white pictures of Ryman Auditorium and stumble across an old ad for O.K. Houck Piano Co. from the 1940s, making a note to look into them when I get to Nashville.

Suddenly, the phone rings, startling me from my thoughts.

"This is Audrey."

I hear Dr. O's voice on the other end, "Hello, Audrey."

"Dr. O! How are you, my dear?"

"Doing well, Audrey."

"Good... good..."

"I've been researching a trip for us. Somewhere we've never been before. What do you think of taking an adventure to Alaska?"

"Alaska? Sounds like fun!"

"Oh great, I'll start making the arrangements. How about the month after Nashville?"

"Yes, after my Nashville trip. That would work well."

"And Audrey, I also was just wondering if you've given any more thought to the question I asked you on the cruise? It's been months, and..."

"I know, I know... I just need a little more time. I know I've said that before, but I promise—in Alaska."

"Okay, in Alaska then. I miss you, Audrey, but I can't keep waiting forever." He really wants an answer, but I'm just not ready yet.

"Mmhmm. I miss you too, goodnight."

I've had Nashville in my sights for a while because of the fascinating music history there. Ryman Auditorium, known for its natural acoustics, was practically the Carnegie Hall of the South. Not to mention the music legends who have performed there. Everyone from Dolly Parton to Hank Williams and even John Phillip Sousa played his first concert there in the late 1800s.

There was a radio show that used to play classical music and opera dating back to 1925 that my father happened to put on at home. I can remember sitting on the floor with my legs crossed, eyes closed, and listening to George Gershwin play "Rhapsody in Blue" for the first time and the smell of mom's mashed potatoes and gravy wafting through my nose. I remember just being in awe listening to the speed of his fingers and the melodic theme that made me want to jump for joy and cry all at the same time. I'd never heard anything so beautiful.

I would look at our piano, which looked so lonely sitting in the corner of our little living room and imagined myself playing the keys as fast and as delicately as Gershwin did. Gosh, I haven't thought about that in years. It's amazing how a song can bring you back right to a moment in time. I want to see that piano, the piano that Gershwin played, an antique Steinway B from 1925 with the black lacquer finish. Nashville was the place to find it.

GRAND OLE OPRY, FALL—1993

I didn't know what to pack for Nashville, but Rose and I had fun shopping to find the perfect red cowgirl hat and brown boots with red stitching. I don't know why I thought that would help me blend in because as soon as I open my mouth, you can hear my North Jersey accent. You can take the girl out of Jersey, but you can't take Jersey out of the girl.

I wanted to spend time by myself on this trip, but the manager at the hotel insisted I take this big Pink Tour Bus run by these two sisters, Shaylene and Dixie Knox, and I heard them before I saw them. The bus was blasting Billy Ray Cyrus as a chorus of strangers sang along to "Achy Breaky Heart," incredibly off-key.

Well, this was going to be interesting.

The bus pulled up to my hotel, Shaylene and Dixie hugged me like I was their long-lost third sister, and I thought maybe the hotel manager knew something I didn't. They made it a point to learn each person's name on the bus and would constantly weave our names into jokes and jabs throughout the tour. Their comic timing was just hysterical, and my cheeks hurt from laughing so hard. We drove by the Farmer's Market, through downtown, Legendary Music Row, the Country Music Hall of Fame, and finally the last stop, the Grand Ole Opry at Ryman Auditorium. I climbed down the stairs of the bus, eager for what I would hope to find next.

"Have fun looking for pianos! We're rooting for you. You damn Yankee." Shaylene and Dixie yell out of the bus.

"Thanks, girls!" I smile and wave back. What a hoot. Now those are two women who don't care what anyone thinks, and I admire their boldness. That's the kind of energy I want to exude.

Another tour guide greets me, who is smiling wider than a Cheshire cat. Her big teased blond hair is bigger than my cowgirl hat, and I can't help but smile back at her. She seems so darn happy to be here, and if I'm honest, so am I. I'm so excited to see this piano.

"Welcome to the Grand Ole Opry! I'm Darlene. How can I help you?"

"Thank you! I was wondering if you could tell me where the piano is, the one that's from 1925 mentioned in this brochure?" I ask.

"Ah, unfortunately, it's been removed for refurbishing. It was really outa tune, and the keys were breaking left and right," Darlene says.

Why didn't I call ahead of time to check and make sure it would be here? I'm kicking myself right now for not doing that. The whole point of this trip was to find this specific piano.

"I see, that's a shame. I came all this way just to see it," I say.

"Just to see an old piano?" Darlene asks. It's not just an old piano to me, though. Darlene clearly doesn't understand the significance and probably could care less about anything that old. She can't be more than twenty herself, or maybe thirty. Ugh, what's the difference? Young is young.

"Well, I'm kind of on a pilgrimage to see pianos all over the world, and this one, in particular, is important for me to see," I say.

"A piano pilgrimage, well, isn't that neat. Do you play, ma'am?" Darlene asks. Ma'am, well, now I feel a hundred. She is sweet, though.

"I do. I've been playing since I was ten years old," I say.

"Well, bless your heart. Now you know, the one from 1925 is being refurbished, but since you play and all, maybe you'd like to see another special piano we do have here. It was played by none other than President Nixon himself."

Nixon. Wow. I laugh to myself thinking of a joke the Knox sisters would say right now, "Three men walk into the Grand Ole Opry to play the piano, Richard Nixon, George Gershwin, and Elvis Presley. Which one of them ends up in jail?" Jokes aside, I didn't come all this way to see a piano played by a president I didn't even vote for.

So, if it's not the 1925 piano Gershwin played, what piano was going to make this treasure hunt feel finished? Would it ever feel finished? The hunt had started off as a whim, a fun excuse to travel not only the world, experience new places, and cultures, and find pianos, but also find the piano I knew I still needed to play. It had also become an excuse to avoid the man who had asked me to marry him.

"Really? That is interesting, but I think I'm ready to head back to my hotel. There's one piano I really need to play, and it's definitely not Nixon's." I don't want to offend her, but I'm not wasting any more time. I know what I need to do.

"Thank you, Darlene," I say.

"You bet. Good luck with your piano!" she says.

"Thank you! But first, I gotta go see a man about a fish."

"You're a strange bird, but good luck with that!"

I have kept him waiting for months, and it's time to face the music. I owe him an answer, and he's going to get one.

FISHING IN ALASKA, ONE MONTH LATER—1993

"So now we wait," I say.

"We just wait?" Dr. O asks.

"Yes, and relax," I say.

I close my eyes and breathe in the beauty and the stillness of this magical place. The air is so clean that as I inhale, my lungs fill with the same smell from a fresh winter morning candle you would normally have to buy in a store.

"We wait and relax," Dr. O repeats.

I'm allowing myself to revel in the silence only nature can bring, when all you hear is the sound of the water flowing, the birds chirping, and the trees quietly acknowledging each other as they sway in the wind. The evergreens surround us as the majestic gray mountains peer down at us with their snowy tips. If there was ever a moment where I wondered what God was doing on the day he created the earth, it's clear he started with Alaska.

"So, exactly how long do I have to wait?" Dr. O breaks my silence, fidgeting with his fishing pole.

"Well, longer than the minute it's been since we put our poles in the water," I reply.

"It's been a lot longer than that," he says.

"We're not talking about fishing anymore, are we?" I knew this was coming. I came here to give him an answer, but the beauty of this place is beyond distracting. I hope the words come out as I've practiced them in my head.

"I've been patient, Audrey. First, it was your trip to Ireland with Rose, then Nashville. It's been months. If you don't feel the same way anymore, just tell me," he says.

"No, no, that's just it. I do feel the same way. I—I love you, Trey. I do." Using his first name feels strange. He's still Dr. O. to me.

"Why don't you ever call me that?"

"I'm sorry, old habits die hard. You were my doctor way before I loved you, and I do, love you, Trey. But I don't need to be your wife to go on more adventures with you. I mean that. I really, really do." I take a deep breath, knowing there's more I have to share. "I can't go backward. I can't go back to being defined by the roles I play and the men and children who depend on me. I choose me. I choose independence, and happiness, *and* love. I don't need a Mrs. before my name to have all those things. I'm just Audrey, and that is enough. I am enough, and I've always been enough."

"Oh, well, now I feel foolish," he says.

"No! Please don't. I want to keep going on adventures with you! But I've been someone's wife, and you've been someone's husband. I don't want that at this stage of my life. I love what we have our independence and freedom."

"I do too. I just thought it would be nice to make it official," he replies.

"Well, it's official to me, and I am officially having so much fun!"

"Me too." I'm relieved how Trey understands I can't marry him. I don't want to lose him, but I also still have my own journey to finish. We smile at each other in agreeable silence when suddenly there's a soft splash. "Wait a minute, what is that?" Dr. O asks. He is tugging on his fishing pole now, trying to hold it steady as it pulls at him.

"It's a fish! Let me help you. This is how you reel it in." I put my hands on his fishing rod and help him reel in the fish. A big pink salmon comes flopping out of the water, squirming to get free. I smile, knowing how that fish feels, and, in this moment, I know when I catch one, I will give her freedom and release her back into the water to chart her own path.

"I got it!" Dr. O exclaims.

"I can't believe you caught one before me. Did I forget to mention I hate to lose?"

"Ha, so do I. Who taught you how to fish anyway?" he asks.

"My brother Bobby. We used to fish down in Rumson all the time when we were kids." My heart hurts picturing him in his youth, with his gorgeous curls, the sun-kissed freckles on his face, and determined to catch more fish than me. He had the whole world ahead of him, and I will never stop mourning the man he never got to become and owe it to his legacy to be an even better version of myself.

"You've never really talked about him. Tell me about him."

"Gosh, where do I start? This one time when we were kids, we carved our initials under the piano to get back at our mother…"

It had all started at the piano with my family, and after all the traveling, I missed home and my family.

CHAPTER 35

IT'S NEVER TOO LATE

AUDREY: AUDREY'S HOUSE, CHRISTMAS—1993

Snowflakes are falling as the car pulls up in front of my house. Dr. O and I said goodbye at the airport so he could go straight home to spend Christmas with his kids, and I could spend it with mine. As I peer out of the glass window, I can't help but feel like I'm in my own little snow globe. With each shake, my memory brings me backward and forward. A small girl wearing a red hat and mittens runs across the lawn, two lovers are ice skating across a frozen pond, a brother and sister are busy making a snowman, and three friends are chasing each other having a snowball fight.

I shake it again, and there's a young mother rocking her daughter to sleep, and then a young father holding the mother as she looks at an empty bassinet. I shake it again, and two middle-aged women are sitting on a bench drinking wine out of a bottle laughing and crying, a stack of letters blowing in the wind, an abandoned piano in the middle of the snow, lined with thirteen little sets of shoes. I shake it one last time and don't let it settle. The snowflakes flurry about as I put it all behind me and open the door.

"Mom! Your home! We have a surprise for you. Come with me," Helen says as I barely have time to put my suitcases down as she helps me out of my coat and hat.

Bernadette links my left arm, and Robert links his with my right as they walk me into the living room. Everyone is here, my children, their spouses, and all my grandchildren. They all look like little Christmas presents wrapped and tied so beautifully in red velvet, hunter green, and adorned with beautiful gold and silver bows. I've missed them all so much in my travels.

I'm distracted by seeing all their warm and smiling faces that I almost miss it. The kids move aside and behind them is the most beautiful baby grand piano I've ever seen.

I know instantly it's *my piano*.

But it looks different. It's sparkling black, and I can practically see my reflection in it, with the biggest red bow I've ever seen wrapped around it. I gasp and approach it slowly like it's an old friend I haven't seen in so long I'm afraid she won't remember me. I sit down at the bench and reach my hand underneath just to be sure.

When I feel the initials, I know it's really mine. I smile widely as tears begin to fall down my face, and I look up to heaven and to Bobby.

"How did you ever find it?" I say, trying to breathe through the tears.

"Aunt Rose searched for it while you were in Nashville and Alaska. With some help from this crazy thing called the internet, she tracked it down, and we all chipped in to buy it. We wanted to surprise you." Robert says.

"And surprise me, you did! That Rose sure knows how to keep a secret. I never thought I'd see this piano again. Thank you, all of you. It's the most thoughtful gift I've ever received," I say.

"We know how much you've sacrificed for us," Helen says. "And we wanted to say thank you. You always filled our house and lives with music. We wanted to give that back to you," Robert adds.

"Music was always your greatest accomplishment," Veronica chimes.

"You know, who's to say what our greatest accomplishments are. I know I've lived a lot of life, I've had a lot of babies, and I've played a lot of music. I have loved a lot, and I've lost a lot, and I had dreams, really big dreams. But sometimes life gets in the way of those dreams; love gets in the way, death gets in the way, even children get in the way."

I look around at my children with a small laugh. "I mean, what am I saying? You're not in the way. You just changed the course of some of my dreams. But that's the crazy thing about life, right? Things change. And why would we want things to stay the same? Where's the fun in that?" I ask as I glance at all the faces around me.

I smile as I notice little pieces of me in each of their faces.

"Your Aunt Rose told me once to keep my eyes and heart open because we think things are going to go in a straight path, but they never really do. Life is messy and complicated. Hell, I'm messy and complicated." I hear my children laugh, a few replying in agreement.

I shake my head and continue. "So, follow the path, and don't be discouraged when it starts to turn in a different direction, because that direction is where you are meant to be. If one dream ends, there's another one headed your way. It might be to a new career, a new love, a new child, a new friend, or like me, a new trip around the world, finding pianos and finding independence. It's never too late to follow your dreams. I know I'm not done dreaming, and let's face it, we dream *big* in this family."

"Yeah, and we're big and loud!" Veronica echoed.

"Yes, big and loud. Now, it's time for my favorite family tradition; show tunes around the piano. Everyone must perform something! Where is my talented granddaughter? Amelia, what show should we start with? *The Sound of Music*? *Miss Saigon*? I do love that new *Rent*, but of course, it's really La Boehme..."

"*Rent*! Definitely *Rent*! I love that you know the hottest show on Broadway, Grandma," Amelia says as she comes up to the piano, I scoot over, and Amelia sits down on the bench next to me.

While Amelia flips through music books deciding what we should sing first, my mind is already wandering to another piano.

"I was wondering if you'd like to go to the theater with me next week?" I ask.

"You had me at theater, Grandma. I'd love to," Amelia says.

CARNEGIE HALL, NEW YEAR'S DAY—1994

"What are we doing at Carnegie Hall?" Amelia asks, eyes wide as she takes in the grandiosity of the empty concert hall.

"I have some unfinished business here," I say as I look out at a sea of empty red velvet seats.

My eyes scan up to each balcony level overlooking the stage with majestic omniscience as the lights twinkle in the darkness. There is a holiness to this place, and I breathe in the air that countless musicians have breathed before me. I quietly take in the beauty around me and smile, thinking of all the places I've been, and yet none of them quite compared to Carnegie.

It's like coming home.

I'm lost in my thoughts when a familiar face walks onto the empty stage, dressed in all black and carrying a clipboard.

"Mrs. Murphy?" Suzie asks.

"Suzie, please call me Audrey," I say.

"Ah, old habit." Suzie laughs as she gives me a big hug.

"Where are my manners? Suzie, please meet my granddaughter, Amelia. Amelia, Suzie was one of my best piano students."

"Nice to meet you, Amelia. Your grandmother is being humble. She was one of the best teachers I ever had," Suzie says as she shakes Amelia's hand.

"I don't doubt that! I hope I can play as well as she can one day," Amelia says.

"That is incredibly kind of you both to say. I was so excited to get your letter that you moved back to New York!" I say.

"Yeah, Australia was an adventure, but I'm not gonna lie, I missed New York something awful," Suzie says.

"I did too," I say, realizing just how much I missed being in this place again.

"So are we gonna just stand around here talking, or are you going to do what you came here to do?" Suzie asks.

"You don't know what this means to me."

"I think I do. The stage is yours," Suzie says as she gives me a wink and motions to the piano set center stage. I see it glimmering at me, calling me to come to play it. My heart is racing, my fingers are tingling, and my stomach is doing backflips.

I traveled the world searching for pianos, and I never dreamed *my* piano would come back to me, but this one I

need to play on my terms. On this stage, on my timetable.
Amelia takes my hand and carefully walks me on stage up
to the piano. "You heard her grandma. The stage is yours. You are never
too old..." Amelia starts.
"...and you are never too young to make music," I finish.
I sit down at the piano, take a big breath, and start to play.
This time for an audience of two, and I couldn't be happier.

It's Never Too Late

AUDREY
It's never too late
It's never too late
To grab a hold of your dreams
It's never too late
To reach for the stars
It's never too late
When the sky seems so gray
It's never too late to try

It's never too late
When the world's gone astray
It's never too late
To start a new day
It's never too late
It's never too late to try!

So, what's holding me back?
What's getting in my way?
I've made so many mistakes
And lost love along the way

I always depended on men
to make my dreams come true
this time it's not up to them
And it's not up to you
It's never too late
To make a new dream
It's never too late
To reach for the stars
It's never too late
When the fear won't subside
It's never too late
It's never too late,
To try

Amelia stands and claps furiously from the empty theater, and I can just see the outline of an older woman clapping alongside her. I know immediately who has snuck in. I had told Rose that Suzie worked here, and we had arranged to be here in between shows when we would have the place to ourselves.

"Bravo! Bravo!" Amelia yells.

"You're a girl. You're Irish. You can do anything!" Rose yells from her seat.

I'm so happy they both are here to experience this moment with me. My past, my present, and my future, all here with me.

CHAPTER 36

EPILOGUE—THE NEXT CHAPTER

AUDREY: NEW YORK CITY, SUMMER—1999

My daughters always joke about what they will do when they outlive their spouses. They say to just put them all in a house together, and they'll take care of each other. I figured I would just stay in my house for as long as I could, but Rose presented a different option.

She reminded me one night at dinner on the Upper West Side, "We went straight from living with our parents to living with our husbands. We never got to be young and independent women living in New York City together."

"You make a very valid point," I said. We might not have been young, but we were finally independent. So, I sold my house in Nutley and moved into Rose's apartment in New York.

We have our tea together every morning out on the balcony overlooking Central Park as we scan the arts section of the paper, deciding what museum, show, or restaurant we should try next. Rose found us a cooking class at a local restaurant, and we each cook one of our new specialties once a week. I've even managed not to make the smoke alarm go off, so who says you can't keep learning at our age! We are having an absolute ball.

We did have to make room for a second piano in the living room, and I've started to teach Rose how to play in the afternoons. She always admired Oscar's ability to just sit and play all the classics, and she's picking it up slowly. I see a dueling piano concert in our future. Speaking of concerts, they are all I can think about these days. I finally get to spend my nights on stage, and Rose is partially to thank for that. She pushed me to audition again.

As I look into the vanity backstage, I think about how incredibly lucky I am to have Rose in my life. I apply some more All-Day Rich and Rosy Lipstick, add a little more rouge to my cheeks, and powder my nose one more time. I hear a knock at my dressing room door, and there she is, Rose with a huge bouquet of red roses and blue hydrangeas.

"Hello, darling. You look fabulous," she says as she gives me a hug and kisses me on the cheek. She hands me the flowers, and I put them down on my dressing room table.

"Thank you! These are beautiful."

"Well, it's not every night I get to see my best friend perform. We've waited a long time for this."

"Yes, we have," I say. "And you did such an amazing job scouting other women in their sixties and seventies returning to the stage."

"It was a brilliant idea for a concert series. I'm just so proud to have been a part of it! There are so many talented women of all ages in this city."

"There sure are. It's never too late, right?"

"Funny you should use those words… I actually have someone here with me tonight."

"What? Like a date?"

"Yes! I mean, I don't want to get married or anything, just have some fun." I can't even imagine Rose dating. She's cut that part of herself off for so long, but how wonderful if she wants to try. We are reversing roles. I remember the thrill of my first date with Dr. O in Little Italy and our cruise together, and I hope she'll have some fun like I did.

"Seventy *is* the new Sixty," I say.

"Exactly."

"We are practically aging backward at this point," I joke.

"We're not exactly the *Sex and the City* girls from that TV program Amelia keeps talking about, but seeing you follow your dreams gave me the courage to put myself back out there again," she says with a glimmer in her eye.

I can feel myself blushing a bit. I caught one episode Amelia was an extra in, and there was *a lot* of sex. Once I got past the shock, I saw how these women were completely devoted to each other, no matter what. True friendship between girlfriends is one of life's greatest gifts.

"Well, we are definitely the two coolest single ladies on the Upper West Side."

"That we are, now go break some legs and sing your heart out."

"That was always the plan. It just took a few detours to get here." I give Rose a kiss, and we both walk out, Rose to her seat in the audience and I to the wings of the stage. The butterflies are circling in my stomach, and I say a little prayer to calm my nerves.

Thank you, Lord, for the journey and the destination. Thank you, Bobby, for believing in me even when I didn't believe in myself. Thank you, Rose, for holding my hand through every dream and every heartache. Thank you, Ted, for being the laughter and the armor. Thank you to the little girl inside of me who never stopped dreaming.

As I wait in the wings, I can hear the buzz of the audience in their seats and can see Amelia, Veronica, Robert, Helen, Bernadette, and the rest of the family in the first few rows, their faces beaming with pride and excitement. The stage is dark except for one spotlight in the center, illuminating the piano. She is the star I will share the stage with tonight, just me and the piano.

I will sing the song I sang the night this dream ripped away from me and when my whole life changed directions. But this time, I'm older, wiser, and I've learned not only to forgive the past but to embrace it because I wouldn't be who I am today without it.

"Ladies and Gentleman, welcome to Carnegie Hall's Concert Series, *Ballad of Dreams.*"

Woman of the Century

AUDREY
When I was a girl
Nothing could stop me
Even when life tried to pull me down
When I was a girl
My dreams were ahead of me

Passion and drive
A brother who loved me
Anything was possible
The girl that I was
loved playing piano

Melody and harmony
That little girl
dreamed of the stage
And at the center was me
Anything was possible
Now I look around

And I can clearly see
each memory shaped
my identity

This is it
This is who I'm supposed to be
This is what I was made for
I'm the woman of the century
I'm the woman of the century

— CURTAIN CLOSES —

ACKNOWLEDGMENTS

———

Thank you, Lord, for the gift of music. Thank you for placing your dreams in my heart and for the opportunity to share those dreams with the world.

Thank you to my husband Al Hernandez for your love, patience and for supporting every one of my dreams. I couldn't have done it without you! To Ollie and Charlie, thank you for knowing how much my musical means to me and for cheering me on through every stage.

Thank you to my parents. My mom, Theresa Swenson, for answering every question about Grandma and your childhood and for your unwavering belief in my talent and generous support! My dad, Sal Garaio, for being my number one fan and for your extreme generosity. To my sister, Vanessa Garaio, for everything from lyric talks to show tunes at the piano with Grandma, 'hit it VV!'

To my Uncle Frank Bigley for your stories, memories, and input on so many drafts of the musical! To my cousin Lauren Thelander-Simons for helping me rename my lead characters! To the whole Bigley family for your love, support, and for shaping who I am today!

To my OG's who were critical in getting this story out of me; Judy Bunker-Zanin, the best Dramaturg, and friend, Rory Hughes, for being as excited about this story as I was, for every call, introduction, and pep talk, and Kerri Lynn Miller for inspiring me with your own work and for your creative support!

Cindy McArthur, for your love and support and belief in me, this story, and music.

Jeremy Konopka-White, Anna Upton, and Nicholas Rodriguez for bringing both the characters and music to life! To the Syracuse and NYC Musical Theater Community who showed up for me with their love, feedback, and talent.

Jerome Kurtenbach, who taught me so much about writing during our COVID Zoom sessions!

VP Boyle, for being the best musical theater coach in the biz, and Michelle Akin, for coaching me through my fear to give birth to a musical book baby.

Marissa Fernandez and Jaime Ellis, thank you for your friendship and support through the most fun and scary transition year!

To my TheaterMakers Studio Writing Group and Eric Webb, thank you for being an important part of my writing journey.

Thank you to the team at Creator Institute and New Degree Press, Eric Koester, Brian Bies, and

Haley Newlin, for all you taught me this year and for brainstorming a new book title I love!

To the sisterhood of women authors who held each other up during this process, especially Neelam Patel and Valeria Aloe, I'm so grateful for you! Katherine White, thank you for your social media support during the campaign!

To my editing team, Jordan Waterwash, your support in transitioning from musical to book was exactly what I needed at the exact right time. Thank you for helping me to become a better writer! To my marketing and revisions editor, Michelle Pollack, thank you for taking my writing to the next level and for all your support!

A special thank you to my family, friends, and colleagues who preordered a copy of my book and donated to my prelaunch campaign. A book, an audiobook, and a soundtrack of the musical would not be possible without each of you and your generosity!

Acasia Olson
Adam Benosky
Alberto Hernandez
Allison Clemens
Alison Franz
Alyssa Hess
Amy Scott
Andrea Caserta
Anna Upton
Annamarie McGannon
Autumn Chapple
Barbara Rabke
Barbara Steele
Beau Worley
Beth DeCicco
Beth DiLizia
Beth Goldman Chakravorty
Breeanna Ebben
Brian Kozub
Briana Nelson

Brian Nocella
Carol Akian
Carol Cucci
Chelsea Lincoln
Christine Aguesseau
Christine O'Day
Christopher Buchanan
Claire Morrow
Clare Gillis
Claudia Monse
Clint Wallace
Cathy Maloney
Colin P. Hanlon
Corey Wexler
Courtney Kaczynski
Cindy McArthur
Dana Fitzgerald
Danny & Roseanne Hernandez
Daniel Barry

Dave Macarone
Debra Gibbons
Deidre Smith
Deirdre Bigley
Diane Teed
Dorothy Biondi
Elizabeth Kuczek
Elizabeth Mahoney
Ellen Carissimo
Ellen Papera
Emily Golden
Eric Koester
Eric Webb
Erin Buckley
Frank & Nancy Bigley
Gabriella Ferragamo
Gail Fernandez
Geoffrey Fitzgerald
Giovanni Morant
Gregory Buza
Heather Stitely
Ian Kevin Scott
Jag Patel
Jaime Ellis
Janice Smith
Jeanie Coomber
Jen Beckerman
Jenna Mate
Jennifer Hinger
Jennifer L Frantz
Jennifer O'Connor
Jeremy Konopka-White

Jessica Spina
Jessica Smith
Jillian Kohl
Jessica Wright
Joan & Ken Gantz
Joe Russoniello
Jolene Vettese
Jonathan Mathews
Jordan Waterwash
Joseph Cuomo
Juanita Yepes
Juliana Peters
Julianna Braunschweiger
Katherine White
Katie Adamiak
Katie Cincotta
Katie Reed
Kelly Peppers
Ken Judy
Kevin Liparini
Kim Gatewood
Kimberly Bertram
Kimberly Dwyre
Krisanne Pook
Kristen B Hubler
Kristen Frohn
Kristen Salgado
Kristina Mangus
Laura Mariano
Laura Sugg
Lauren Garlewicz
Lauren Gioino

Lauren LoPorto
Lauren Thelander Simons
Leah Lichy
Leigh Weinman
Linda Jenness
Lindsey Morse
Liz Hahn
Lori Bogin
Lori Schak
Lynn Boyer
Maria & Grayson Murray
Marianne Bruu-Syversen
Marie Kozub
Marisa Budwick
Marissa Fernandez
Marisa Shapiro
Mark & Ruth Bigley
Mary Jakubowski
Maryanne Spatola
Marybeth Febus
Matt & Mary Beth Bigley
Maura Charles
Megan Schaaf
Melanie McDowell
Melissa Garaio
Melissa Navarro
Meredith Hamilton
Micah Burge
Michelle Akin
Michelle Westfort
Mindy Lvoff
Miranda Cogswell

Mollie O'Brien
Myka Meier
Natalie Loeb
Neelam Patel
Nicole Lovullo
Nola Solomon
Owen Gantz
Pam Marini
Patricia Thelander
Penny Lane Hoeppner
Pierina Lametta
Poyee Chiu
Rachel Dyana Grainger
Rachel Gordon
Rebecca Braitling
Robb Sapp
Robert Malone
Rory Hughes
Ryan Pearce
Sally & Paul Almeida
Salvatore Garaio
Samantha Breger
Sara Pedersen
Sarah Caffrey
Sarah Ciancarelli
Sarah Hadzima
Sarah Murchison
Sarah Spencer
Shannon Decker
Shawn Devine
Shira Ginsberg
Sophie Swietochowski

Stevie Sparks
Sue Covelli-Buntley
Susan Bohan
Susan Ross
Susan Silverman
Suzanne Borgognone
Theresa Swenson

Tina Bonito
Virginia Posluszny
Valeria Aloe
Vanessa Garaio
Violet Koehler
Virginie Aris

APPENDIX

—

AUTHOR'S NOTE

Documentary Central, YouTube, 2020, *"Hamilton: One Shot at Broadway, 2017,"* Video, 1:13:49 https://www.youtube.com/watch?v=WGrwiDxWEI4.

Garnett, Laura. *The Genius Habit.* New York: Sourcebooks, 2019.

CHAPTER 8

Spirit of St. Louis 2 Project. "Charles Lindbergh America First" Last modified 2014. http://charleslindbergh.com/americanfirst/speech.asp.

CHAPTER 10

Psalm 34:18 (New International Version).

CHAPTER 29

Jeremiah 29:11 (New International Version).

Made in the USA
Middletown, DE
12 January 2022

58489782R00179